The Polyhedric Mirror
Tales of American Life

JOSÉ RODRIGUES MIGUÉIS

The Polyhedric Mirror
Tales of American Life

Selection, Translation and Introduction
by David Brookshaw

Gávea-Brown
Providence, Rhode Island

Author: José Rodrigues Miguéis

Original Title: This volume is an anthology of Miguéis' American
          chronicles.

Translator: David Brookshaw

Cover: Jesse Costa

Publisher: Gávea-Brown Publications

          Department of Portuguese and Brazilian Studies

          Box O, Brown University

          Providence, RI 02912

Distributer: Luso-Brazilian Books

          560 West 180th St. Suite 304

          New York, N.Y. 10003

® 2005 by Gávea-Brown Publications and David Brookshaw

Library of Congress Control Number: 2005939135

ISBN: 0-943722-34-9

Acknowledgement

This book was published with the support of the Camões Institute, Portugal.

Esta obra foi publicada com o apoio do Instituto Camões, Portugal.

Table of Contents

INTRODUCTION

F or a nation that has witnessed the departure of so many of its
native sons as emigrants over the past few centuries, it is perhaps surprising that the theme of emigration should be so poorly represented in the literature of Continental Portugal. I stress 'continental',
because the opposite is true in the literary history of the Azores, in which
departure, migration, and the diasporic condition have become central
to its focus. It is, of course, true that great national literary figures of the
nineteenth century, such as Almeida Garrett, went into exile for political
reasons, and Eça de Queirós spent much of his life as an expatriate.
However, as a diplomat, he remained a functionary of the Portuguese
State. Eça was intellectually and culturally cosmopolitan, but not a migrant. In the twentieth century, both Miguel Torga and Ferreira de Castro
based some of their fiction among immigrant Portuguese communities
in Brazil, having themselves experienced immigration at a relatively early
age. However, they both returned to their country of origin and went on
to write about other themes. The same could be said, more recently, of
Olga Gonçalves. The notable exception within twentieth-century Portuguese literature is José Rodrigues Miguéis.

    Born in Lisbon in 1901, Miguéis was the youngest of three chil-
dren, the son of a Galician migrant father and a mother whose roots lay
in the Coimbra area. His childhood was spent in the heart of Lisbon's
Baixa (downtown), and even though the family moved to a home on the

recently built Avenida Almirante Reis, thus suggesting a degree of social ambition and mobility on the part of his parents, most of his life until he left Portugal revolved around central Lisbon, with its literary cafés and vaguely bohemian human scenario. This was the Portugal he remained emotionally attached to throughout his life and the one evoked in his novel, *A Escola do Paraíso* (1960).

It was while studying law at Lisbon University between 1919 and 1924 that Miguéis became actively engaged in democratic and republican organizations. Of particular significance, in this respect, was his collaboration in the review *Seara Nova*, which had been founded by Raul Proença, Raul Brandão, and Jaime Cortesão in 1921. Miguéis contributed articles and cover illustrations to the publication and maintained contact with the *Seara Nova* group even after he left Portugal. The mid-1920s saw him working as a lawyer, with occasional spells in a notary's office, but he also sought a position as a secondary school teacher. In fact, it was his interest in pedagogical matters that eventually led him to obtain a government grant to take a degree in education at the Free University of Brussels, Belgium, between 1929 and 1933. There is little doubt that his experience of living in the center of Europe, against the background of a rising tide of fascism, from which Portugal, of course, was not immune, helped to loosen his ties with his home country. This, and an unsuccessful marriage to a woman of Russian Jewish origin, who was unable to adapt to life in Portugal, thereby causing their separation, led him to contemplate the possibility of emigrating. In 1935, helped partly by his future wife, Camila Campanella, a woman of Portuguese and Italian extraction who had lived in New York since she was a child and whom Miguéis had first met in Lisbon in 1928, he left for the United States, where he would live virtually uninterrupted until his death in 1980.

His motives for emigrating to the United States were, therefore, as has often been suggested, mixed. If possible personal disillusionment, coupled with an experience of foreign travel still fresh in his memory, were sufficient reason for leaving Portugal, this was almost certainly rendered more desirable by the consolidation of Salazar's power in 1933/4 and the establishment of an apparatus of state repression that was to victimize many left-wing intellectuals like Miguéis over the next forty years.

Among Miguéis's extensive array of work is *Gente de Terceira Classe* (1962), which was translated into English, along with several other short tales, under the title of *Steerage and Ten Other Stories* (1983). This was the first collection of stories made available to an English-reading public, which focused largely on the lives and aspirations of Portuguese immigrants in the United States. The present collection of stories, chronicles, and essays is intended to pay further homage to Miguéis's power not only as an observer of immigrant and expatriate life, but as a commentator on modern urban American society and culture. The first two essays in this book are taken from *É Proibido Apontar – Reflexões de um Burguês I* (1964). Among the longer stories, "Trading with the Enemy" was first published in the *Diário de Lisboa* in 1971, as was "The Happy Christmas Story I Didn't Write" in 1966. Both were included in the collection, *Comércio com o Inimigo* (1973). "Bon Voyage, Carlos" and "Agnès – or an Asexual Love" appeared in the *Diário Popular* in 1980. All of them featured in the later collection of short stories, *Paços Confusos* (1982). "The Arrival", dated 1980, was found among the author's personal documents in the John Hay Library at Brown University in 2002, and was subsequently published in the Portuguese literary magazine, *Ficções* (2003). However, the bulk of the tales and essays chosen here are from the collection *O Espelho Poliédrico* (1973), which is why the latter title has been preserved in English. Indeed, every effort has been made to reflect the spirit of this title in conveying a sense of the variety and the multi-faceted nature of Miguéis's depiction of everyday life in New York, the city where he lived for over half his life.

One of the most abiding comments made by the appreciators of Miguéis as a writer in Portugal is his 'portuguesismo', or strong sense of identification with his Portuguese roots, in spite of his long absence from his native country. The supreme expression of this, according to his commentators, was that he always wrote in Portuguese, in spite of the fluency he gained over the years and the fact that he often resorted to English words and terms (preserved in italics in the translation), not to mention occasionally anglicizing his Portuguese. On the other hand, as one critic points out, he never failed to write as a Portuguese:

> It is a Portuguese gaze that R.M. passes over this vast world, a gaze that is concerned, even to the point of crucifixion, by the *idea* that others may have of us and – above all – even by the degree to which they confer an existence upon us, not merely as individuals, but more fundamentally, as *Portuguese*.[1]

What is perhaps more interesting about Miguéis and undoubtedly a feature that adds to the uniqueness of his work, is the fact that he in effect became a writer of the diaspora, assuming many of the intellectual characteristics of a man of two worlds, or between two worlds. In the words of one critic, he combined the reflexes, attitudes and emotions of the exile, the expatriate and the emigrant.[2] The ambiguities that emerged in his writing as a result of this add to its richness. In "There Is Always a Bey in Tunis", he is, for example, understandably defensive against negative stereotypes of the Portuguese that he detected among the North Americans, Spanish and Latin Americans with whom he came into contact, and equally proud of what he claims was the least intrusive form of European imperialism: the Portuguese tradition of race mixture throughout its colonial domains, and enshrined in the Luso-Tropicalism of the Brazilian sociologist, Gilberto Freyre.[3] Elsewhere, however, he is equally prone to denounce color prejudice, assumptions of superiority, and cultural pretentiousness among Brazilians and Goans of mixed descent, as in "The Bow-tie" and "An Indian Polychrome" respectively, as well as the provincial nationalism and defensiveness of certain sectors of the Portuguese middle class during the isolationist years of the Salazar dictatorship, as in "Bridges of Dreams". On the other hand, Miguéis was more acutely aware of the advances made by black North Americans during the middle years of the twentieth century than the Luso-Tropicalists, for whom the United States constituted the negative opposite of Portugal and Brazil in the matter of race relations, would have given credit for. His thoughts on the subject, as expressed in "The Black Man and Mr. Harding", were first published in the Portuguese evening paper, *Diário de Lisboa*, in 1971, at a time – and perhaps this was no coincidence – when Portugal was obstinately struggling to maintain its colonial position in Africa.

In other ways too, Miguéis became the interpreter of American social customs for a Portuguese readership. In "Love American Style", some of his assumptions may seem a little dated, but we must remember that Miguéis was born and brought up at the beginning of the twentieth century in what was still a profoundly patriarchal society. What does emerge from this essay on gender relations in America, with its gently ironic and humorous comments about contrasting Latin values, is an overall sympathy for female emancipation and understanding of the issues at stake for both women and men in the expectations society had of them. Many of the points raised are still topical. The same could be said of "His Majesty the Automobile", which is a poignant reminder of the environmental price paid by Western industrial societies, led by the United States, for their dependence on oil, the motor vehicle, and road transportation.

It is in shorter recollections that Miguéis captured the binary opposites in American social and cultural values that so fascinated him for being distinctive, particularly in relation to those of the Latin world. "Weekend '37" describes a trip to a famous artists' colony at Yaddo in the Catskills Mountains in upstate New York,[4] where Miguéis observes the enjoyment middle-class city dwellers derive from being in the bosom of Nature. He comments on the relative freedom with which women disport themselves in the sunshine and is particularly drawn to the way small communities of professionals from the city have organized themselves, building and restoring holiday houses with their own hands. It is this practical way in which Americans enjoy and control the wilderness, a relic perhaps of a pioneering settler spirit, that Miguéis contrasts, either implicitly, or through the thoughts of a Mexican male companion, with the more illiberal, hierarchical Latin tradition. At the same time, the writer's sense of irony leads him to surmise that in their organization of a community, these urban country dwellers have brought some of the preoccupations of city life with them. As for Nature, it can be unforgiving and even murderous when tampered with by mankind, as is nearly the case in "Holiday", a suspense-laden recollection, dressed up as a tale, centered on a family's experience while out boating on a lake and which causes the narrator to briefly ponder on man's vulnerability in the face of death. In two further stories, "The Man Who shot Down the Hindenburg" and "A Tale of Fish", the Nature/Civilization dialectic is viewed from different perspectives. The first is a surprisingly complex piece that, apart from revealing the author's abhorrence of Nazism, ponders on the vulnerability of seemingly unassailable technological advance in the face of a quirk of Nature, whether this is static electricity–one of the possible causes of the Hindenburg accident–or a look of hatred shortly before it exploded. On the other hand, "A Tale of Fish" is a parable on the resilience of the natural world in defying mankind's selective attempts to control it, but it is also a delightfully ironic vignette on a cultural paradox that preserves the lamprey as both beauty and beast, delicacy and predator from the murky depths of rivers and lakes, and a motive, in Latin countries at least, for petty corruption.

Indeed, paradox seldom goes unnoticed by this observer of his fellow men. As a resident in one of the most impersonal and sophisticated metropolises in the world (albeit not without profound problems of social inequality), in a nation of unbounded technological progress and optimism, Miguéis is often drawn to the way its citizens react when the unexpected happens. In "A Night of Panic Failure", when the city is left for some hours without electric power (Nature is perhaps once again getting its own back on Civilization), the citizenry demonstrate a capacity to organize themselves in such a way that the expected anarchy and opportunity for crime offered by the incident do not materialize. Similarly, in "A dead Hack", passers-by in the street pause in their rush to try to revive a man who has suffered a heart attack: human society is sufficiently resilient to adapt to rapidly changing circumstances, as the providers of first aid give way to the women who accompany the stricken man in the ritual of death.

Some of the most vivid pieces in *The Polyhedric Mirror* are the tales and evocations of migrant life, with which Miguéis identified so closely. Occasionally, the identification is such that author and narrator become confused, veering between third- and first-person, as in "Holiday", or in the final ironic empathy of the author with his character in "The Man Who Shot Down the Hindenburg". The effect is that what apparently began as a short story ends up masking a recollection, an autobiographical fragment. On the other hand, we must never forget that Miguéis was not an immigrant in the sense that many of his uneducated countrymen were, that is, an economic migrant in search of a better life. On the other hand, he never really achieved, or indeed sought a position of economic security that might have turned him into an American suburban dweller. In many ways, he continued to live the hand-to-mouth bohemian existence he had been used to in downtown Lisbon, but in the Lower East Side of Manhattan, earning his crust as a translator for press agencies and for the Portuguese-language edition of *Reader's Digest*. His contacts and friendships were diverse and not constrained by social boundaries. He supported the republican side in the Spanish Civil War and wrote for *La Voz*, the mouthpiece of the exiles from Franco's Spain. He was also actively involved with the Portuguese immigrant community, helping to found the Clube Operário Português, an association that enabled him to feel that he was contributing to working-class solidarity, in accordance with his political ideology. Through his work as a translator, he encountered Latin Americans and Brazilians. All these different groups feature in his recollections. "In the Boarding House" and "A Chimpanzee Called Dorothy" focus on the lives of Portuguese immigrants, underlining at the same time the profound sense of solidarity but also personal isolation because of class difference that Miguéis felt in relation to his compatriots. Indeed, isolation and hardship, the need to survive and the intelligence bred by necessity among many of his migrant countrymen were a source of admiration for Miguéis, ultimately causing him to overlook behavior or cultural preferences that seemed to rub against his own social and political principles. Thus, Carlos's hackneyed taste in Anadalusian Flamenco music and Lisbon Fado, in "Bon Voyage, Carlos", is forgiven in favor of recognition of his lonely life of adventure and dislocation. In many ways, Carlos, the sailor who went native in Samoa, the man of many loves, and the fervent reader of Camões, is the twentieth-century embodiment of the Portuguese heroes of old. Similarly, Taveira's currency speculation and smuggling in "Trading With the Enemy" is admired in the context of this immigrant's warmth and generosity towards his fellow men. It is undoubtedly true that the practice of survival in the land of the American Dream tempered the sharper edges of Miguéis's Marxist ideological commitment.

On the other hand, "Bertico" and "The Bottle of Brandy" both focus, with humane irony, on two of the more colorful Hispanic acquaintances Miguéis made among the *demi-monde* of exiles, while "The Chastity Belt" highlights the gulf in understanding that often exists between the immigrant in the defense of his social mores and the host culture. Other tales and chronicles, such as "Linoleum '36", "Retrospection," and "On a Visitor's Visa," describe incidents of latent violence, either on the part of the authorities or of individuals, which seem to underline the vulnerability Miguéis felt as a foreigner in a strange and potentially hostile environment. If these are earlier recollections of his time in New York, there is evidence that he never felt, nor ever wanted to feel, totally integrated. "The Happy Christmas Story I Didn't Write" is a meditation on the question of identity, which extends to the problem of writing and the motivating force behind writing, which Miguéis had always attributed to an ideological commitment. Surrounded by the commercial and consumerist values of the American metropolis as he wanders through the streets of midtown Manhattan at Christmas time, Miguéis feels a profound sense of alienation and powerlessness, and yet at the same time, he seems to come to the reluctant but interestingly postmodern conclusion that identity is not an absolute condition but an arena in which competing values struggle with each other. In many ways, then, this tale is Miguéis's most explicit discourse on cultural pluralism and its effect upon him as an outsider (but who, by the 1960s, was also an insider) and as a writer and a man with a political pedigree rooted in the anti-Fascist opposition of Portugal in the 1930s.[5] However, whatever his sensitivities with regard to his own sense of emotional and ideological alienation, his position was never as dire as that of the down-and-outs he evokes, with a sympathy worthy of Steinbeck and Dos Passos, two of his American literary models, in "Bowery '64", which contains a vivid description of one of New York's older poor quarters.

During the four decades Miguéis lived in the United States, he found himself adapting to numerous changes brought about by the formative influences which surrounded him. If his left-wing sympathies were incompatible with the overwhelming power of American capitalism, he also found it hard to adapt to the relative sexual freedoms encountered in New York's advanced urban civilization. Nowhere is this confrontation more apparent than in "The Arrival". Written at the very end of his life, it is a strongly autobiographical tale that the fictional names of the protagonists scarcely disguise. It corresponds to Northrop Frye's definition of autobiography as confession, describing the first weeks of his re-encounter in 1935 with the woman who had sponsored his move to New York and who would later become his wife. It is a candid tale about the vulnerabilities of a young Portuguese man propelled into the bohemian circles of Greenwich Village, which turns into an examination of the jealousy felt towards his lover and the way he eventually manages to come to terms with this, if not entirely overcome it. One of the sexual fantasies the ingenuous young Latin male in "The Arrival" has is of being able to turn a lesbian into a consenting heterosexual–the supreme proof of his manhood. This, then, forms the basis of "Agnès–or an asexual love", in which an old man's fantasy becomes a dialogue on the nature of sexual love as understood differently by men and women.

Over a period of forty years between 1935 and 1974, the year that witnessed the end of the Portuguese dictatorship of which Miguéis had been an outspoken opponent, transport between the Old World and the New had been revolutionized. If he had left his homeland on a transatlantic liner, by the end of his life, the same journey could be accomplished in a matter of hours by passenger jet. There is little doubt that Miguéis could have returned to Portugal if he so wished. However, in spite of his attachment to his roots, he could never re-forge the links with Portugal where, to his regret, he remained largely unrecognized. The link between the expatriate and his native land remained fraught with contradiction, the type of obsessive nostalgia and paranoid resentment that is expressed through characters like Carlos and Taveira. Perhaps that is why this most original of Portuguese writers never managed to "go home", but continually returned to the anonymity of Manhattan, which he had grown irreversibly used to, even if he never quite learned to love it as his own. He died there in 1980.

In bringing this project to fruition, I should like to thank Professor Onésimo Almeida for his unstinting support and encouragement as I continually found new material to add. A word of acknowledgement is due to Mark Brown, at the John Hay Library, Brown University, for welcoming me and other colleagues on the occasion of the Sixth Congress of the International Lusitanists' Association in July 2002, and showing us the Miguéis collection, and then for sending me so promptly a copy of the manuscript of "A chegada". Thanks too to Luísa Costa Gomes and Zé Lima, in Lisbon, for their interest in publishing this *inédito* in the review *Ficções*. Translating Miguéis is a challenge; his style is often elliptic, rich in its expressiveness, and I am indebted to my colleague, Madalena Pires, here at Bristol, for her helpful advice in clearing up some of the doubts I had. Finally, I embarked on this project shortly after my wife, Celeste, and I visited New York in the autumn of 2001. In wanting to re-visit the Greenwich Village she remembered from visits to the city in her youth, she inadvertently led me in the footsteps of Miguéis. My thanks to her.

David Brookshaw
Bristol, United Kingdom
December 2003

Select Bibliography

A) Translations of works by Miguéis:
Steerage and Ten Other Stories, Providence RI, Gávea-Brown: 1983 (Ed. with a Foreword by George Monteiro). *A Man Smiles at Death with Half a Face*, Hanover and London: University Press of New England, 1990 (Translated with an Introduction by George Monteiro).
B) Critical monographs or collections of essays on Miguéis:
Almeida, Onésimo T. (ed.), *José Rodrigues Miguéis: Lisbon in Manhattan*, Providence RI: Gávea-Brown, 1984. Almeida, Onésimo T. & Rêgo, Manuela (eds.), *José Rodrigues Miguéis: Uma Vida em Papeis Repartida*, Lisbon: Câmara Municipal de Lisboa, 2001.
Kerr, John Austin Jr., *Miguéis–To the Seventh Decade*, University of Mississippi, Romance Monographs 29, 1977.
Neves, Mário, *Vida e Obra de José Rodrigues Miguéis*, Lisbon: Editorial Caminho, 1990.

C) Internet sources on Miguéis:

http://www.brown.edu/Facilities/University_Library/libs/hay/collections/
    migueis/
http://www.instituto-camoes.pt/escritores/migueis.htm

Notes

[1] Eduardo Lourenço, "As marcas do exílio no discurso de Rodrigues Miguéis", in Onésimo T. Almeida (ed.), *José Rodrigues Miguéis: Lisbon in Manhattan,* Providence RI: Gávea-Brown, 1984:41.

[2] Domingos de Oliveira Dias, "J. Rodrigues Miguéis: O homem e o círculo", *Gávea-Brown*, vols. XII-XIV, Jan. 1991-Dec. 1993:18.

[3] Gilberto Freyre (1900-87) was Brazil's leading social historian of the first half of the twentieth century, with pioneering studies of Brazilian slave society, such as *The Masters and the Slaves* and *The Mansions and the Shanties*. His studies of Portuguese integration in the tropics led him to coin the term 'Luso-Tropicalism', that was appropriated by the ideologists of the Salazar regime during the 1950s to justify Portugal's colonial presence in Africa.

[4] Raymond Sayers, "The America of José Rodrigues Miguéis", in Almeida, op.cit.:34.

[5] For a lucid appraisal of Miguéis's sense of dislocation, see Eugénio Lisboa's essay, "Ouro e prata em terra estrangeira", in O.T. Almeida, & M. Rêgo, *José Rodrigues Miguéis – Uma Vida em Papeis Repartida*, Lisbon: Câmara Municipal de Lisboa, 2001, pp.151-156.

There is Always a Bey in Tunis

Can it be that the people of a particular country have the reputation they deserve? What elements come to play in the image that the rest of the world forms of them, and then retains? For many, England is a nation of shopkeepers; Shylock still symbolizes the race of Israel; the Spaniard is an arrogant little squire; the German, a robot-soldier; the Frenchman, a mustachioed fellow who has no knowledge of geography but has been awarded a decoration, loves wine but is a miser; and the North American is a missionary with the manner of a traveling salesman.

In vain do we resort to the Greece of Pericles in order to understand and respect the Greek of our own age: the stereotype we are given of him is that of a sailor and an unscrupulous trader. Superimposed over the image of Dante's and Michelangelo's Italy in the view of the man in the street on the other side of the Atlantic, is that of the Calabrese or Sicilian immigrant, of the effeminate warbler of opera, of the St Louis or Chicago gangster, or the New York racketeer.

All these images contain a measure of truth and falseness, of the sketchy and the simplistic; but the common man thrives on the association of ideas to a far greater extent than he does on fundamental truths, and this explains the power of such mundane conceptions. And it is almost always for their defects and weaknesses rather than for their virtues that the people of different countries are viewed, that is, when their subjective virtues are not objectively taken as vices.

The Australian anthropologist Robert Briffault wrote, in *The Decline and Fall of the British Empire,* that the ideal of a nation's character or type of culture becomes fossilized in the tradition of the most glorious moment of its historical development. Following this theory, the Portuguese prototype is still rooted subjectively, albeit with an overdose of disillusion and bitterness, in the Portuguese of imperial tradition, who carried with him an ecumenical dream of hegemony and monopoly, even when he could neither read nor write. However, the image that others have is the one etched on their minds as a result of their encounter with him at the crossroads of history, or the one found on their world travels, like the flotsam left on the beach by the ebbing tide. The conventional image given to us at school–the personification of the Faith and Empire, the geographer and navigator–has largely been dismantled as it has given way to the fortune hunter and trader, the individualist in search of quick profit who seeks a living wherever he can find one, who is active and sober but who rarely has any flights of imagination or inventiveness, almost always giving precedence to the expedient over what is durable, indifferent to the color of skin under which Venus manifests herself, clever and cunning but devoid of any real finesse. In a word, the country bumpkin who took to the sea in order to save his belly from the effects of poverty. Along with this, in the higher social strata, we have the fellow who is presumptuous and conscious of the pedigree of his surnames, which he drags around with him like a string of memories.

It's the popular stereotype I am talking about here, not the one that may hover in the placid air of learned libraries. The pirate, the braggart, the slaver, the rough old salt, the smuggler and bootlegger, the sentimentalist who veers between the easy laugh (*The Portuguese are always jolly, whether up a tree or under the holly!*) and the excruciating uterine melancholy of "fado"–that is the stereotype of the Portuguese who have dispersed throughout the world. In addition to this, he is an example of an "impure" race: a miscegenized-miscegenator. Many foreigners, upon meeting a Portuguese with light skin and fair hair, make the following observation: "But you don't look Portuguese!" What sort of Portuguese is it, whose ready-made, preconceived image has stuck to their retina? Not to be dark or black, dusky or olive-skinned is not to correspond to what is commonplace. In vain does one point out that if you cross Portugal, or even Lisbon, you will find more people with light-colored blue-gray or blue-green eyes, than in the Babel that is New York. A Jewish lady friend of mine was astonished by the number of "Jews" she encountered in Lisbon; and she even became quite alarmed at the way they stared alluringly at her with their gray eyes, silently propositioning her. As far as she was concerned, the typical Portuguese had a pale, golden complexion, with curly, dark blond or brown hair. Even I am astounded to see, for example, among the "wild ducks" or itinerant workers on Lisbon building sites, so many intense green eyes, so many red faces and fair or ginger hair: what is the origin of this racial stream that is so different from the Portuguese norm?

In spite of this light-eyed Portuguese of almost certain Celtic, Swabian or Visigothic descent, about whom Paulo Prado wrote in his well known essay on "Brazilian sadness", it is the figure of the Luso-African that persists in the world, and whose mixed origins predate the period of expansion and even the foundation of the nation. This is the figure that Gilberto Freyre accepted out of love for easy concepts that seem to explain everything in themselves (without in fact explaining anything at all), just as Oliveira Martins had adopted the man of Semitic influences in order to explain our national messianic spirit. But in that case why not talk about the messianic soul of the Spaniard, or of those countries where the Jew lived for thousands of years, or of those where he was more hospitably received? Should that which explains things here not also explain things elsewhere? Why, when it comes to the Portuguese sailor or colonial in the tropics, does everyone discern traces of the Moor (apart from anything else, what is a "Moor"?), while no one mentions him when referring to the Spaniard or the Italian from the south of the country, especially the Sicilian, all of whom experienced for much longer and on their own doorstep, the presence or dominion of the Islamic African? It is true that the North Americans regard any dark skinned, mestizo, or racially ambivalent person as "Spanish" or "Latin", anyone, that is, from south of the Rio Grande.

The Portuguese of the United States react against this African image of themselves. Is this because they have been contaminated by a cultural environment in which anti-black prejudice is stronger than in Portugal? Or is it out of fear of seeing themselves more or less closely associated with the colored races? Many American visitors to Cape Cod, in Massachusetts, return home thinking that the Portuguese are colored; this is because there are many Cape Verdeans in the area who, even when completely black, proudly proclaim themselves Portuguese, or at least they used to.

The black people of Trinidad used to sing:

Go to Madeira
And there you'll see
Portugee belly full of flee.
Portugee he
Portugee she
Portugee belly full of flee.

Brazil alone has created an entire folkloric tradition based on the satirical figure of the Portuguese, and even many of its best living writers resort to the figure of the *portuga*, with his mustache, selling fruit or greens, sleeves rolled up his hairy arms, who builds a block of flats for renting out over his corner shop, and ends up marrying his daughter, complete with dowry, to a local graduate, given to poetry and sweet talk. As far as all his new relatives are concerned, he will always be the *galego*. Unmistakably Brazilian, too, is the caricature of the Portuguese drooling over fiery mulatto women (and who in Brazil doesn't drool over them?), or taking a black woman as a lover. Yet might not this be one of the contributing factors in the legitimate pride celebrated Brazilians have taken in their racial tolerance and in their "authentically mixed" culture? (The outstanding Brazilian journalist, Rafael Corrêa d'Oliveira, told me that whenever someone talked to him about the aristocracy in Brazil, he always recalled that saying about one's ancestors having one foot in the kitchen and one in the bush–the black nanny and the elusive Indian woman.) Without the Portuguese, unfussy in matters of color, where would this all be?

The Spanish Americans, in spite of the prestige of Eça and the repu-tation enjoyed among them by Oliveira Martins, Junqueiro, Antero, Eugénio de Castro and Pascoaes, have the most absurd ideas about the Portuguese. Some of these have almost certainly reached them from Brazil; others persist from Castilian prejudices that gave currency to certain peculiar stereotypes of the Portuguese. In Venezuela (and I imagine in Colombia, too), a "Portuguese" was an unscrupulous trader and a syn-onym for a Jew. (Professor Charles Boxer, in his biography of Salvador Correia de Sá, refers to Jewish merchants who were, or at least said they were Portuguese, and who played a significant part in penetrating the interior of South America. Buenos Aires was founded by Portuguese, many of them probably New Christians, and the trail to Potosi, across the plains and the foothills of the Andes, was dotted with Portuguese (or so-called Portuguese) adventurers, intent on attracting the traffic in silver to the city on the river to which the metal gave its name–the River Plate.)

Unamuno gave the Spanish, in *Por tierras de Portugal y España,* and in a well known sonnet of Sebastianist inspiration, a figure gleaned from a certain period in Portuguese life, steeped in the Satanism of Junqueiro, the pessimism of Oliveira Martins and the sadness of Manuel Laranjeira; this figure even spread as far as North America, where Don Miguel is much read and admired. A *portuguesada,* in the Spanish-speaking world, is the same as *une espagnolade* or *galéjade* for the French, and also for the Italians. We don't have a monopoly when it comes to bravado!

In the United States, when a Spaniard meets a Portuguese, he is almost certain to give him a puzzled look, as if he had not encountered the "creature" he expected to: *"Ah, so you're Portuguese then? Now, I've been told that the Portuguese call a parting in the hair 'flea avenue' and bed bugs, 'boudoir panthers'!"* Another little expression that makes them fall around laughing is our term "belly of the leg" to describe the calf. I have found myself having to explain to various Spanish speakers or Spaniards, some of them teachers, that "belly of the leg", which is an anatomic metaphor comparable to so many others in current use, came straight from the Greek, whose term for this salient, rounded muscle is *gastrocnemio…* So whether or not the designation is ridiculous, blame for it must be apportioned to anatomists with a penchant for showing off their Hellenistic origins.

Another story they like to recall in jest straight away is the one about the battleship *Adamastor,* "terror of the oceans". Some, more erudite, recite the following to us:

A fellow from Portugal
Thought it a miracle
That kids in France so young
Were fluent in their native tongue.

"Why the devil should it be so?"
he said, twirling his mustachio,
"that to talk like a gent
an old Portuguese still makes mistakes
whereas here a child has what it takes."

As if this were not enough, the honorable Galicians of Lisbon used to say: "We've come here to sell them the water that's already theirs!"

The talented Ramón Gómez de la Serna claimed (possibly inspired by Teófilo) that Don Quixote was a caricature of the swashbuckling Portuguese Cervantes had met, lugging his ragged cape and his rusty sword round the taverns of the Mediterranean; if that's true, how blessed he was by inspiration!

The Peruvian novelist, Ciro Alegría, once told me, with scarcely concealed pride: "The Portuguese discovered Brazil, but it was Orellana, a Spaniard, who first sailed down the Amazon!" To which I retorted: "It was harder to sail upstream than down; and it was the Luso-Brazilians who sailed up the Amazon and took the frontier of Brazil as far as the Andes!"

My learned friend, Angel Flores, now a teacher at Queen's College, Long Island, in the days when he was a typical denizen of Greenwich Village, once blurted out the following cordially hostile comment after we had had a few beers together: "It took a Portuguese from Madeira to come to the United States for them to be able to boast they had the greatest novelist in the world!" He was referring to John dos Passos, who was then at the pinnacle of his fame and totally indifferent to the fact that his grandfather was Portuguese.

If the Spanish smile at the mention of the Portuguese, the Italians become sullen, for from Mussolini through to his most illustrious opponents, Portugal is an English "factory house", and all of us to a man, "the lackeys of England". Meager consolation for the unfortunates of the ephemeral *Impero*, to tread on the bunions of their more modest, but in some ways, more fortunate kinsman!

Let us leave aside the mental picture our Latin brothers have of us, which is often dictated by a morbid desire to emulate (but dead things have a tenacious ability to survive!), or by fierce competition among ethnic minorities within the bosom of the great, victorious nation, aimed at currying favor and preferential treatment. Instead, let us see what our Anglo-Saxon friends think of us. The subject is inexhaustible, and I shall not claim to do any more than scratch the surface.

The British also turned the sharpness of their humor as rivals against the Portuguese, but in this case they were more favored by the whims of fortune. If, on the one hand, they always saw the Portuguese as a slave trader or slave owner, on the other, it was they who disseminated the pejorative image of him as a sort of "mestizo". English literature was to create a certain type of Portuguese–an adventurer, pirate, an intolerant bigot and plunderer of treasure–for which the image very possibly served as an initial model. It's not enough to unseat a plutocrat; he must also be discredited before the eyes of the world.

(For example, it is common to attribute the positive aspects of Portuguese maritime discoveries and conquests to the New Christians; but when it comes to imputing responsibilities from a critical perspective, then it is the "real Portuguese" who get the blame. Thus, the sugar planting civilization of the New World was the work of the Jews, but the hateful practice of slavery, without which sugar cultivation, from Brazil to the British West Indies would not have been possible, is blamed upon Portuguese slave traders. And who, indeed, wouldn't have participated avidly in the great international business venture of the age?)

Yet it was an olive skinned Portuguese who inspired Thomas More in his celebrated *Utopia*; what supreme glory, as if that of Don Quixote was not enough! (André Maurois gives us a modern reincarnation of this olive complexioned Portuguese, in the shape of the pedant, M. de Portalegre, in one of his novels of the First World War.) This image of the Portuguese comes right down to Charles Nordoff's *Mutiny on the Bounty*, and as far as I know, has its most recent fleeting appearance in a short story by the prematurely deceased American poet, Stephen Vincent Benet; it is the tale of a Portuguese corsair who starves to death all alone on a desert island in the Pacific, as he gazes in delirium at the treasures he hid there, his nest egg, the fruits of a life of pillage on the high seas. It's like some forgotten page from *Peregrinação* or the *História Trágico-Marítima*.

We might recall at this point one of the most vitriolic anti-Portuguese books, *The Bible in Spain*, by the famous author and peddler of the Gospel, the Englishman George Borrow, for whom all that was mean, selfish, and narrow minded was Portuguese, while anything Spanish, including the beggars in their rags, was noble and generous. On reading it, one has the impression that even the bed bugs in Spanish inns were pleasant. Even in the marvelous pages of William Beckford (who left us perhaps the only living description of Bocage and the Abbot Correia da Serra), there are depictions of the life and character of the Portuguese that correspond exactly to the stereotype. In one of the popular musical comedies by Gilbert & Sullivan, there appears a character by the name of Gama, who embodies, with psychological subtlety, a very Portuguese characteristic: the killjoy habit we have of telling people the truth to their face at an inappropriate moment. Nevertheless, it is worth noting that in the History of Civilization that Mr. Nehru wrote in letters addressed to his daughter while he was in prison, he makes solemn and respectful reference to the actions of Portugal in India.

That picture of the Portuguese as an adventurer, a morally decadent conquistador, or as a beachcomber gone native, stems without a doubt from the encounter on what I shall call the "periphery of contact" of the victorious and better equipped Anglo-Saxon with the Portuguese–many of whom were mestizos or even natives who, in their own decadence and weakness, had assimilated certain superficial features of Portuguese culture. And it was natural that they should turn up pretty well all over the world, from the shores of America to Africa, and from Hawaii to the remotest parts of Melanesia: *Portugee belly full of flee*…I remember the deep impression made on me when, as a boy, I read a book published on the occasion of a centenary, in which there was a study of Portuguese influences in Ceylon. Portugal was there for less than two hundred years, and yet, three centuries on, people there still sang popular songs such as "Papagaio Louro". Among the many initials of the Prime Minister, Mrs Bandaranaike, there is a D., which stands for Dias.

These mestizos and natives who have assimilated the culture of the once or still present ruling power, often take greater pride in their Portuguese descent than Mr. John dos Passos; this is the case with the Cape Verdeans of New England, who often guard their Portuguese identity, not to mention their good manners, far more jealously than many light or even tawny eyed Portuguese, who turn their nose up at them. (The famous "bishop" Grace made a fortune out of a religious sect he founded among Black Americans. He was a Cape Verdean by the name of Graça.)

To diverge for a moment, in this question of skin color, educated Portuguese are like the Russians who take pride in their mulatto (or was he a quadroon?) Pushkin. The Portuguese who feels humiliated because "racist" Anglo-Saxons and others confuse him with the vast range of mestizos that our people spawned throughout the world rejects the greatest and maybe the only truly enduring virtue to have emerged from the process of Portuguese expansion: the relative absence of segregation or racial hatred, that which Jaime Cortesão generously termed "Christocentrism". But it is good to show caution in our impulsive claims to being a nation of traditionally benign customs; it was Dr. Pangloss who said that everything has its logic or essential truth, and we Portuguese had some reasons to breach racial barriers, making a virtue out of necessity or weakness, among others were certainly the scarcity of people to work the land and man the imperial defenses. In cultural terms, although we may occasionally have descended to the level of those who are poorer than we are, or we may have distorted our original character, the result has nevertheless been a positive one; that the Amerindian or the African may have to some extent been considered people gifted with a soul, and as such susceptible to conversion and salvation, is certainly a step on the road to progress, in relation to the more rigid beliefs of others, for whom the only good Indian was a dead one, and who preferred to massacre rather than convert them. If there is a certain cultural patriotism in this, it is worth remembering that all peoples and all ages have contributed in their own way and in some measure to the good–as well as to the bad–of humanity.

A large North American dictionary includes under the heading of Portuguese, apart from the synonym for foreigner, *dago*, etc., the word *Melungeon* (*mélangeon*? French), which in the old days was the term used to describe the people of mixed Indian, Black and White descent in Tennessee. The word *Portagee*, or *Portugee* (pronounced poragui, poregui) are also pejorative. Let us hope that one day, now that relations between the United States and Portugal are getting closer, it may be possible, by means of a solemn exchange of diplomatic notes, to strike out from that useful old tome, the root term that so offends the pride the sons of Lusus take in their "racial purity".

And while we are barking up this particular tree, let us pick out one or two more casual examples.

Mrs Vera Kelsey, the author of crime novels, many years ago published a little book called *Seven Keys to Brazil*, where among other enormities she says, despite all that she learnt or failed to learn with Gilberto Freyre, that during the colonial period in Brazil the Portuguese were so "backward" that they had to import blacksmiths from Angola so that they could be sure of having people who knew how to work iron. Now it is a well known fact that Africans have been skilled metal workers for a long time; but among Mrs Kelsey's "seven keys", the Portuguese key is clearly missing, and this is the one that would have opened the door to her understanding of Brazil. Let us hope the good lady is more successful at finding the "keys" to the mysteries in her crime stories!

Another lady traveler whose name I have forgotten, writing in a New York magazine devoted to fostering commercial relations with Brazil, declared her surprise at finding what seemed to her to be "strange Chinese influences" in the architecture of the city of Salvador (Bahia); then, ignorant of the Portuguese roots of Brazil and the binding link established by Portugal between Asia and America, she went on to describe what was in effect our colonial Baroque. On the other hand, why should we be surprised by this, when a well-known Brazilian, upon showing me one day some statuettes or religious images from Minas Gerais, truly Portuguese in style, told me they were authentic Brazilian pieces of art?

The great singer and black leader, Paul Robeson, also affirmed that when the Portuguese first visited the African coast in search of slaves, gold, and ivory, they had a much more rudimentary social organization than that of the black tribes with whom they made contact. But whether it is to praise the intensely original character of our kindred Brazilian culture, or to exalt the incontestable qualities of the African and repair the injustices of which he has been victim, both before and after having had contact with the Portuguese, it does not strike me as necessary to insult those colonizers most given to miscegenation.

At an important general meeting in a Hollywood studio, they were putting the final touches to a film that was about to be shot, when someone objected to the fact that the villain of the story was a Mexican; they were at war and in full pursuit of a policy of good neighborliness, and Mexico–a neighbor, good friend, and ally–might get offended. So what nation could he be attributed to, then? The discussion continued, until a clever typist suggested they take a look at the list of countries that bought films from the company. On checking, they saw that the fortieth and last country on the list was Portugal, a tiny market, and the villain, to everyone's great relief, suddenly became Portuguese.

In the novel, *My Sister Eileen*, by the witty Ruth McKenney (an expatriate in England now for many years), there is a group of young cadets in the Brazilian navy, who fulfill the not always desirable role of "romantic lover", commonly attributed in the United States to "Latinos": *"Latins are lousy lovers..."* The novel formed the basis for a very successful film comedy during the war years. But Brazil–a good neighbor, friend, and ally–had joined the conflict, and once again the same problem emerged: would the Brazilians be offended by the innocent caricature? In a flash, the "romantic" sailors became Portuguese.

At a certain point in an argument with her boyfriend, in the film *Primrose Path*, based on the novel of the same name by E. Ellul, the blond Ginger Rogers tells him heatedly: "Who do you take me for? One of those *Portugee girls?*" The "Portuguese girls" she was referring to, ugly dark-skinned hookers from low dives, are of course played by females of another nationality who, in order to make themselves pass for *Portugee*, speak a distorted version of Castilian... Come now, Ginger, my good lady! The Portuguese of California are good, humble, hard-working folk, maybe sometimes a little on the coarse side, often prosperous, modest, and God-fearing, and with low crime rates; they don't deserve such scorn from such a pretty mouth!

Our "countrymen" are delivered another slap in the face by John Steinbeck in *Tortilla Flat*, a delightfully told pocket-sized Don Quixote; it is an amusing human story about a group of mestizo Hispanics in California, cunning, roguish, philosophical, and when God wills it, pilferers. For the purposes of comic contrast, he needed to include in the group a primitive character, devoid of humor, who was at once a simpleton, clumsy, and a scapegoat, and Steinbeck made him Portuguese: *Joe Portagee*.

The most glaring case, however, can be found in a novel by a lesser writer, LeGrand Canon Junior, who, to portray the embodiment of ill will, brutishness, and the total absence of sporting behavior, in contrast to the elegance and honesty of the 'Nordic man', chose a Portuguese–Joe Felipe, *Black Joe Portugee*. The story is set in New Hampshire and in 1729 (when there certainly wouldn't have been any Portuguese in that territory). Two village lads, one of pure Anglo-Saxon stock, the other a Portuguese, compete for the affection of the only available girl, who hesitates between the two of them. In order to settle the dispute, she decides to subject them publicly to a hay-cutting contest. The Portuguese–with his tangled black hair, bull's neck and powerful torso, in other words the prototype of the villain or 'bad guy' in films – gets off to a better start; but his rival, calm, methodic, and athletic (this in 1729), gradually pulls ahead. On seeing this, Black Joe, in his exasperation, hurls his scythe at the back of his rival's knees so as to mutilate him… He feels the full weight of all the villagers' anger, is punished and chased out of town, while the slim Galahad conquers his chosen maiden's heart.

The novel was published in an abridged form in *The Reader's Digest*, but I opposed its publication in the Portuguese language edition, thereby risking my modest job and salary as an editorial assistant. "But I deleted the word *Portugee!*" My friend Eduardo Cárdenas, the chief editor assured me. "It won't cause anyone offence." To which I replied that the caricature of all that was hateful was a "darkie"; and the hero was blond, wide shouldered, and slim of hip, like today's athletes, and I added: "Seeing as we are at war with the racists personified by Lohengrin, this story is racist. Do you know what people in Latin America and the rest of the world will say tomorrow? That here we are waging war against Lohengrin, in order to proclaim the superiority of Lohen*gringo!*" We both laughed, and the summary of the novel went straight into the waste-paper basket.

While on this subject, my friend Leo Pap, who has been doing research on the Portuguese in the United States for many years and without any official backing, and who published at his own expense an interesting book on our language as it is spoken there, told me that he had written to the author of this drivel, inquiring about his historical sources. The fellow replied saying it was all fiction, that he had only ever met one Portuguese in all his life (in Connecticut), and as for the existence of Portuguese in New Hampshire and in that remote period, many years before Independence, he had never heard anything to support it. Of such things history is made, and above all legends!

It is very rare that the role of the Portuguese is acknowledged, for example, in the history of the United States navy; the famous frigate, Bonhomme Richard, with which the patriot John Paul Jones harried the English, in the first display of American naval power, was crewed largely by Portuguese sailors, no doubt from the Atlantic islands. Moreover, it is well known that the Portuguese of New England played a pioneering part, as captains and crew of whalers and sailing ships, in trade between New England and the Pacific. Aboard the Acushnet, the whaling ship on which Herman Melville gained the experience that would enable him to write the classic, *Moby Dick*, there were at least three Portuguese seamen. One of the names that feature in the book, Cabaco, could well be the most democratic Cabaço or Cavaco.

This history does not appear in the schoolbooks or even in scholarly treatises. But the Portuguese play a leading role in the popular novel, *The Great Waters*, by J. Berger. In the short story, *The Country is Full of Swedes*, by Erskine Caldwell, there is passing mention of the virtues of the Portuguese in Maine, where in fact they do not abound.

At most, to attenuate the coarseness of the popular stereotype, the Portuguese are attributed with certain positive character traits–sobriety, loyalty, and kindness– although permeated by aggressive impulses or an idiotic, primitive ingenuity. It is the case with films like *Tiger Shark* (in the person of lead role played by Ed. Robinson) or *Captains Courageous*, based on the novel by Kipling (in Spencer Tracey's main character), and which the Portuguese rush to see and applaud in great numbers, always grateful for some meager praise and ready to spend their money, thereby making it pay.

The treatment given to the Portuguese in world literature, and especially to that in English and Spanish, in itself constitutes a fascinating topic, sufficient to challenge the patient scholar who is endowed not only with sympathy, but a critical spirit, capable of interpreting it in light of historical relations and conditions.

It remains to be seen to what extent this predominantly scornful stereotype is the fruit of ill will, ignorance or negligence, or of objective observation; also to what extent it is the product of an uncultured mentality that unfortunately characterizes this "Portuguese for export" everywhere he goes, more concerned as he so often is with the priorities of the moment than with lasting values, and as a result of which outsiders then tend to deliver a collective judgment upon us all.

It stands to reason that all peoples follow the path they have chosen or have had imposed upon them. The Portuguese have been neither better nor worse than others, but have committed comparatively more mundane acts and displayed more faults, which is an inevitable consequence of having spread to the four corners of the world and given their bodies to show for it. This is why they carry the burden of their wandering epic destiny, of which Camões and Fernão Mendes Pinto are its quintessential representation, and the *Soldado Prático*, *Peregrinação*, the *História Trágico-Marítima* and the *Arte de Furtar* its most expressive written testimony. We must never forget that the *Peregrinação* was one of the most widely read books of its age in Europe, and the powerful images it left among its readers, along with the day-to-day impressions that the poor sons of Lusus have been scattering throughout the lands and islands of the globe for the last four hundred years, are not of the type that are easily erased.

Rarely are the Portuguese awarded the brief but justified recognition for the good that they have done. However, no one misses an opportunity to denigrate them for the bad acts that they, like others—and sometimes only others—have carried out. Is this because they are weak or largely unknown? Is it because they have no one to defend them? Or is it perhaps because they do not know how to look after their deeper interests, and because they forget that culture is the supreme form by which a people perpetuates itself? I don't know.

When people feel the need to insult, to unleash their irritation, attribute faults and mistakes, certain that they will not be answered and that their interests, alliances and friendships will not be threatened, or quite simply when they are at a loss to know what to talk about, then the Portuguese get hit. Just as in Eça's chronicle, "there is always a bey in Tunis", and there are plenty of Portuguese scattered round this world of ours, with wide and humble enough hides to put up with the blows without complaining.

Love American Style

This little six-year old boy goes out for a walk, hand in hand with his little girl friend from school. He kisses her candidly and solemnly. Maybe he casts himself in the role of her protector, ready to allow himself to be punched on behalf of his lady. At the age of ten they will go together to the corner shop to have a soda or an ice cream. They have begun to feel shame at the idea of kissing each other. Later on, as adolescents, they will go to the cinema together, or drive around in a fourth or fifth-hand jalopy. Contact begins early, and with it gentlemanly manners, gallantry, respect (albeit incomplete) for the "weaker" sex. There are marriages that began like that, in childhood, without any infidelity, although with the occasional sulk. But as a general rule, these friendships lead to various partnerships, because it is not considered good to limit oneself to only one source of affection–*to go steady*.

The ritual extends throughout life: the wealthy man gives his beloved a mink coat or a motor yacht, holidays in Florida, the Bahamas, Newport or Europe, a house on Fifth Avenue, or a thick portfolio of shares in his company. *Courtship*–carried out with gallantry–is an essential rule of etiquette, of accepted moral and cultural values. The man places his strength and his money at the service of the woman, seeks to attract her affection and indulgence with the security of his uncontested superiority. He allows her pre-eminence (*ladies first*), satisfies her desires and whims, and gives her a glimpse of independence, triumph, and prosperity.

To extort a woman's sympathy or consent, to fascinate her, to force her to surrender to her troubled feelings, are all unacceptable; it is not enough that the *lady must be willing*, she must also be in complete control of her faculties. So there is no room for the exaggerated, provocative, or languid gallantries that men resort to in other climates when they look at, follow, or greet the passing female. We don't see him walking along the street with a plea for love hanging from his neck like a beggar's box. An obsession with love is considered a weakness unworthy of the male. Brought up independently and used to man's respect, the woman repudiates the "lady killer", whose clammy, dominating manners always conceal a suggestion, a proposal, and as often as not a threat. She views the man who pays excessive attention to his *toilette* as a male model, an effeminate or a gigolo. (Dressing well, with natural simplicity and rigorous hygiene, is another matter. The American man, like his counterpart, spends a considerable amount on *toiletries*: cologne, shaving lotions, deodorants, and the rest.)

What she appreciates is the man who is assiduous, enterprising, and helpful, devoid of arrogance and not too persistent: a good-humored virile male, who is able to feign to perfection that all he wants from her is dispassionate friendship, and who treats her with a mixture of courtesy and familiarity, concern and deference, desire and self-restraint. Urbaneness is the rule, and the American cultivates to a high degree, sometimes to the point of exaggeration, good manners, which he studies through manuals on etiquette of the type by Emily Post, which has sold millions of copies and gone through numerous editions. Although kissing, *petting*, and *necking* are widespread and practiced by mutual consent from an early age, "hanky-panky" is out of the question. On the other hand, the ruddy-complexioned gentleman who introduces himself in the lift because there are ladies traveling in it, if he meets one of them at the party on the twentieth floor, won't hesitate, after a second drink, to invite her for "tea" or to see the *etchings* he has in his apartment; these are euphemistic and time-honored formulae. But the woman has a right to express her preference; consent to courtship is an indispensable condition. The man is a persistent suitor, but must accept rivalry and rejection like a sport, without rancor or scorn. He must be aware when he has lost the game. Any attempt on his part to impose himself or to express reproach implies sanctions and even risks. The morality, the law and the courts of this masculine society are all organized in the common cause of defending "women in all their fragility."

Nowhere in the world is the number of women one sees so imposing, nor so overwhelming the number of pretty ones. Between five and six in the afternoon, on this or that avenue or street in central New York, it's like an invasion of amazons, a flood, a cataclysm. The outsider feels stifled, in danger of being crushed, victim of some violent act... But, oh, no, these tall, bustling temptresses pass him by without so much as the favor of a glance. They dress well, with elegance and freshness. If they lack a dash of sensuality and the touching allure that distinguish the more bashful Latin woman, the cult of female charms is universal, and even excessive, purposeful, and provocative. Nor is this surprising if the man is so reserved! They throw their beauty in his face as if challenging an iceberg. (A recently married young man told me that the difficult relations between the sexes were due more to the conventional moderation of men rather than to the resistance of women. Could it be that he feared falling into the snare?) Fashions, beauty products, advertising, all masculine creations and inexhaustible sources of revenue, insist on praising woman, on educating and encouraging her to make herself more attractive, the ideal of all men. Everything seems organized to impel the male to desire her. Personal appearance, *sex appeal*, is the main instrument of conquest: in the workplace, in promotion, in getting a husband. And why should men complain of this, if feminine charms are the palliative for a hectic, relentless existence? The constant presence of women in all spheres of activity, but above all in the offices that fill these skyscrapers, gigantic pulsating aviaries, or cliffs inhabited by burrowing creatures, breeds a general climate of tension, which is all part of the anxiety, the stimulus, and the indefinite promise in which America vibrates ceaselessly. Cinema, theater, reading, opportunities for jobs and profit, wealth or mere survival in comfort, the automobile that gives us the illusion of being able to go everywhere, no matter how far (and has transformed the once immobile woman into an audacious and dynamic lover), the overwhelming vastness of the surroundings that threatens to separate us irredeemably one from another (maybe tomorrow will be too late!); this excitement, this laughter, this exuberance, this dizzying activity–all seem to awaken within us the fervor of a brimming vital, genetic impulse. It is as if, all of a sudden, a hidden, diabolical force has scattered through the air the seeds of an endless desire, an overdose of erotic frustration. It is the carrot, eternally dangled in front of the donkey's nose, but always unattainable.

This feeling sometimes gives rise to an almost ferocious outburst of sadistic cruelty, in which the poor male is deliberately tantalized. That slender girl, with narrow hips, meager breast, and square shoulders, that hardened temptress, brimming with health, almost asexual, but embellished with all the technical resources of beauty, radiates an unquenchable attraction and seems to have only one desire or pleasure in life: to drive men mad and subject them to the most atrocious of privations. She does not inspire tenderness; she instills brutal impulses to possess and dominate, to torture and crush, like the "Apaches" in relation to whores. She is the *vamp*, the "femme fatale", the *gold-digger*, the victor. For her are the millions, the gaudy posters, the multicolored glossy magazines, the shops full to bursting, the expensive furs, the automobiles made to order. But will she ever overcome her frigidity and quiver with love? Whatever the case, for her, love is a battle, a duel based on hatred, like the *two-backed beast* of the Poet.

Salacious tales about sexual provocation are common currency. (The puritanical *Reader's Digest* publishes the sauciest stories in all the American press.) What do these folk do who stream out of theaters and clubs of the more "burlesque" type, nude bars, striptease joints (an art that consists of slow, ritualistic undressing to the rhythm of an orchestra), where provocation reaches the point of obscenity, the violence of flagellation and masochistic submission? What did they go there to learn? Does this most basic form of enticement by any chance engender complete satisfaction? There is something perverse in all this, something that runs against Puritanism (or its corrupt body), and that leaves the European bewildered. This abstinence in the midst of excitement, this suppression of explosively intense desires, suddenly strangled or diverted from their natural course, produces an anger and melancholy, a complaint that pervades the country's great and lesser literature alike; for all we know, they may be the cause of these outbursts of uncontained anger, alcoholism, recourse to homosexuality and drugs, aggression and suicide, that suddenly take hold of men, women, and adolescents, not to mention the violence and perverse crimes of which women are almost always the exclusive victims.

Maybe all this has only one aim: to channel this mass libido towards marriage and virtue–and above all, towards all powerful business interests.

Indeed, for Anglo-Saxon culture and morality, demonstrating one's strength, resisting instinctual urges, this is the supreme proof of virility. Even the kiss, the screen kiss, the kiss that epitomizes America like the advertisements for Coca-Cola, is a derivative, a substitute, an obstacle on the road to satisfaction. Behind this apparent debauchery, there is a certain prudishness, a formality in libertine behavior. The woman prefers a man who is able to resist, to dominate his own impulses and passion; and she no doubt encounters a certain refined pleasure in provoking him, in being courted assiduously. If she is occasionally seduced by the languid Latin, with his "bedroom eyelashes", or even by the low-life gigolo (who, according to the malicious at heart, she seeks out on European tours, as if she wanted to break a fast), once she has regained her composure, she prefers her sober companion, with his good humor and ability to go through long periods of abstinence and to sustain a solid friendship. She is more interested in romance than in the gratification of her instincts. Maybe she is right; perhaps the man who is ever eager to possess is not always the ideal male, the lover with the greatest *endurance*. He is certainly not the most faithful: *Latins are lousy lovers!* And fidelity, if it is not general in this part of the world (far from it), is nevertheless an ethical imperative, a rule of mutual respect. Isabel Duncan, who was no blushing maiden, speaks of the phlegmatic Anglo-Saxon, cold in appearance, but skilled enough in bed to give a faun of Classical Mythology lessons in lovemaking. And in this matter, women must be the supreme judges.

This busy, anxious, solitary man in the great metropolis–the "John Dos Passos man" as I call him–seeks refuge, tenderness, some intimacy and enjoyment; his is a mixture of infantilism in search of his mother's breast and of repressed vigor and sensuality. She is one of so many women who, in the evening, after a day of intense and responsible work, we see in one of these middle-class restaurants, eating her dinner alone, with a magazine or book open in front of her, holding a lit cigarette and absent-mindedly stirring her coffee. She swallows the fruit of her independence, which is not always possible to reconcile with the joy of living and loving, within a vast and as yet immature social framework. Before going home she will maybe go to the cinema to dream a little. After scrupulously seeing to her nightly *toilette*, she will fall asleep round about eleven o'clock, eleven thirty, while reading her novel. Perhaps she feels a frustrated maternal instinct to give of herself and to protect.

One night, these two solitary individuals meet. They swap some polite comments about a book or a film, then, on an impulse, some confidences, a "maybe"... They go for a drink. They will go to a theater together, to a museum, to a concert at Carnegie Hall. Today, tomorrow, some day, there will be some spark of risqué humor between them, some understanding without any sentimentality, a moment of unexpected intimacy. They are both *nice*, worthy, decent people. They love each other, with just a trace of apathy. And so what? They may get married or never see each other again. Or they'll remain friends; they'll meet up from time to time, then, resigned, go their separate ways, he taking the subway to the opposite side of town, she returning with a sigh to her apartment. Maybe he is in an unhappy marriage; and she, if she is not separated from her husband because of irreconcilable interests, is perhaps too busy to devote herself to the sovereign task of making a man happy, of bearing and bringing up children. A postcard, a telegram–"Are you coming on Saturday?" "Impossible, I haven't got time." There's no time to be happy. How far everything is, how short one's leisure hours, how scarce time is, how extreme one's loneliness and endless one's fatigue, how hostile winter, how exhausting the heat of summer! The struggle is a harsh one, life is intense, and love hurried. Lonely, embittered, downtrodden, stoical. This is the price paid for a career, for efficiency, for social mobility and security. But the triumph, when it comes, if it comes, is intoxicating and makes up for all the frustration.

Or else there is the traveling salesman, a cynic, or the bohemian artist or writer, touched by skepticism, averse to conventions or ethical responsibilities: he drinks like a character out of Hemingway or Dashiell Hammett, is used to sniffing out easy women, the "weak" ones, and has a proposal of love hovering on his lips, moistened with sensuality and whiskey. He makes love and moves on–at most, the relationship lasts a couple of months. The woman who abandons herself to him is mad about literature or vain enough to think she can make a huge "conquest", considers herself emancipated, and is hungry for sensation; deep down, she is in despair, dissatisfied, she seeks to stifle her low self-esteem, the frustrated dream of marriage, or fear of it, and she too drinks, has nervous breakdowns, and sees a shrink.

This other woman reads novels of dubious quality, with sensationalist covers, gossip magazines of the "tell all confessional" type (with particular emphasis on film stars and matinée idols), or body-building magazines, with photos of strong men, muscular monsters. She looks at clandestine photos given her by a sailor or the cashier at the record shop, she goes to see morbid films about nudism or kinky sex, she has whispered conversations involving dirty jokes and is obsessed by the rituals and practice of "love". Maybe she's cold, frigid, a frustrated, complex woman, and she tries to solve her problem through fantasized love triangles. Take care! She's capable of cruelty and infidelity.

Yes indeed, there's many a free, uninhibited and unfettered woman out there. "In New York," a female friend tells me, "there's much more lovemaking going on than you can ever imagine. Behind these dark, hermetic façades, these closed curtains and blinds, the sound of love can be heard howling in hushed tones…" The police patrol the crowded squares, keep a watchful eye on high-spirited young girls, anxious couples, and the restaurants in the vicinity of the hotels where depravity seeks refuge. From the bar inside, *call-girls* beckon the passers-by. The war has left its trace of urgency and misbehavior. On dimly lit park benches, couples and threesomes court one another silently and without moving. The violent and theatrical kiss travels at eighty kilometers an hour on the subway. There are inscriptions, invitations, pornographic graffiti on the walls and pillars of the stations, sometimes accompanied by a telephone number.

But what I really find touching are the young girls who toil all week in offices and workshops, God knows how badly paid, and who, come Saturday night, descend *en masse* on a Times Square glittering with lights, with attractions, with promises, with dizziness and illusion, in search of a little fun, a romantic moment of freedom, a boy-friend, a laugh, a kiss in the shadows, a clutching of hands. Who is the woman, and especially a young girl, who doesn't like to hear the words "I love you", whispered by way of homage in her ear? It may all end today, it doesn't matter; better to have memories than to grow bitter with an ever-frustrated desire. This is called an "experience". At heart, the dream is always the same: a romantic courtship, a beautiful wedding, with a photograph of the bride's dress, a loving, busy little husband, a nice home, children one day. Humanity is the same everywhere. "Love is the same the world over," my Viennese psychoanalyst friend tells me. "Only the cultural accessories differ depending on the standard of living and the traditions. Men seek satisfaction and relief, and women seek emancipation, marriage, to have children and to live in relative security. America isn't an exception to the rule!"

A foreign diplomat tells me about a maid of his who had what we call a "lover". But she was engaged to another. "Don't you do the same thing with your fiancé?" the diplomat asked her. "Lord no! With him, it's serious; I intend marrying him." Is this mere hearsay?

With the passing of youthful lust, thoughts turn to setting up home. I ask a writer friend of mine why Americans get married. After an astonished pause, he answers: "To have a faithful, steady companion, I think." Companionship is the fundamental aim of marriage. Marriage is conceived as alien to Tolstoy's drama of carnal obsession, purity, jealousy, of sensuality unsettling affection, confidence and solidarity. Marriage is a sensible union, designed to lead to rational procreation. But what if one is ambushed by some extra-conjugal passion, some upsurge of voluptuousness and intoxication? "Ah! Well, when there is true respect, everything is forgiven!" I know of husbands out there who accept their wife's libertine ways with good natured tolerance, as if it were some sort of illness: and it is. But there is divorce on the grounds of "marital breakdown", mental cruelty and goodness knows what else.

A husband is required to be faithful, energetic, sober, and helpful. A wife (if they don't intend having children straightaway) wants to hang on to her job. The need for independence survives into marriage. Once the children have grown up, the wife who abandoned her career or business many years before, returns to the fray. For example, it is surprising how many mature women, many with silver hair but still looking trim, one encounters in the narrow canyons that make up the thoroughfares of the Wall Street district. But it is not always possible to reconcile the biological and moral responsibilities of a wife and mother with those of a public and professional life. (It is a well-known fact that women doctors, possibly more so in America than in Europe, generally end up single.) Very often, in addition to traditional prejudices and material difficulties, the ideas of personal freedom, the pursuit of happiness and fulfillment of one's ideals learned at school and through reading become exacerbated, and this in turn means that domestic harmony becomes precarious and is put at risk. Sharing one's life with someone requires sacrifice and self-denial, and here it is almost always the man who makes most concessions; if women have made inroads outside the home into the traditional domain of male economic activity, albeit not to the extent that we imagine it to be, he for his part, sees himself taking on functions that were traditionally the preserve of a wife or of domestic servants. But I see them accepting these tasks with happy resignation; among the middle class, although the housewife still has overall responsibility, domestic chores are shared in recognition of marital harmony, the married couple being a team that remains united in love, in the control of temper, and in solidarity. There are people leading exemplary lives, in which there are never any outward signs of passion, but which are perfect or almost so. (In poorer families, especially among the proletariat, whether this consists of Americans or immigrants still clinging to their European values, the woman is still by and large responsible for the housework, which is often added to a harsh and poorly paid job in a factory, a workshop, or domestic service.)

It is assumed that a woman has had (although this is rare) every opportunity to choose an appropriate man–which, of course, doesn't mean that she doesn't make mistakes or end up disappointed. Many extol the virtues of living together before marriage, which in fact is widely practiced. If a man falls in love, the solution is to get married, and generally speaking he fights hard to make it come about. Although in New York, for example, illicit unions are very common, given the Catholic rigors of the law, which only allows divorce in the case of adultery, women don't willingly lend themselves to this situation, for they have their pride and their dream to fulfill. Up until a short time ago, the unwritten law, that is, *Common Law*, recognized and allowed for a *de facto* union that had lasted for some years. In the wealthy upper classes, the ceremonies leading to marriage–the girl's social debut, engagement, betrothal, honeymoon–have all the pomp of a biblical or great social event, as much as or even more so than in Europe. The more humble classes mimic them as far as possible, to the point of absurdity and beyond. A wedding with a solemn cortege, page-boys and bridesmaids, a banquet in a huge hall, a master of ceremonies conducting the ball in accordance with pre-established hierarchies and orders, is one of the most morally disturbing events I have ever witnessed. To what depths of convention people will plunge in the belief that they are on the way up!

The "emancipated" attitude is almost exclusively the preserve of the middle classes, the intelligentsia, and more recently the young, those of the rebellious age groups which have earned the name of *hip* or *beat generation*, and who, in a sense, have taken the informal to the lengths of formality. And so one could say that marriage has lost little if any of its traditional solemnity, and in some cases it has even found added refinement in it.

But love at first sight, the "it-took-just-one-look" syndrome, and fast-track marriages are still frequent occurrences. Social encounters are fortuitous, and attraction, as well as antipathy, breeds quickly. These impulsive, trusting folk, who love surprise, make sudden decisions. Sometimes, after the flight, abduction or elopement, the innocent young things awaken from the effects of alcohol or the orgy and rush to seek an annulment of their hasty marriage, on the grounds of "incompatibility".

The way life is generally organized, the abundance of things, the economic prosperity and relative confidence in the future, in jobs, in the justice system, in welfare in times of sickness and old age, etc., everything conspires to facilitate marriage. In general, the man is not a poor wretch tormented by the problem of balancing his domestic budget, and the woman is not paralyzed by life in the home. All that remains is for them to love each other, and know how to get on together… which, as it is everywhere, is a problem of "upbringing" and of tolerance.

In a climate of hectic work schedules and limited living space, such as occurs in large cities, the difficulties of raising children and educating them within a modest budget are considerable. People voluntarily limit the number of children they have, in spite of the opposition of certain religious groupings to birth control. If the large families of Lincoln's times are tending to disappear (but of course among blacks and Puerto Ricans, for example, birth rates are phenomenally high), here as in other countries, this is counterbalanced by very low rates of infant mortality: the modern family, reduced in numbers, is also healthier and more robust, and individual life expectancy is much longer. Children, conceived in accordance with a planned family, are born overwhelmingly in springtime. The generally held ideal of *the pursuit of happiness*, sanctified by the Constitution, has turned illness into a type of monstrosity to be fought by all possible means; in some states, there is a compulsory prenuptial medical examination because of the fear of syphilis. There are a multitude of heavily publicized campaigns against cancer, poliomyelitis, cardio-vascular diseases, countless forms of paralysis, muscular dystrophy, kidney conditions among children, psychosis, and goodness knows what else. "TWO out of every five men traveling in this carriage will die of cancer!" A poster exclaimed, pointing a threatening finger at me. "Help us combat it!" Next to it, the flaming broadsword of the new crusade… (These terrifying appeals are tending to disappear, but on the other hand, the campaign against smoking is accentuating the fear of illness and death.)

Marriage, like all real personal contracts, is subject to corrupting influences. Invitations to pleasure, wealth, personal initiative, are helping to undermine the time-honored institution. Economically and morally less dependent on each other, freer and more self-sufficient, married couples are no longer willing to compromise when faced with disagreement, which is sometimes of a purely personal nature. Nevertheless, divorce is most common among the wealthy, or film stars, who are handsomely paid, absorbed in their work and in their triumphs, or too depressed to accept the responsibilities of married life. Money buys everything, so people say, but it seems to get in the way of love; or at the most, it provides the means to purchase the illusion of it. Film stars live in a world of exhibitionism and provocation, narcissism and the flattery of appearances, where physical beauty pays well, and they are therefore more open to the temptations of a promiscuity that thrives on the feeble majesty of ritual and on publicity. But there are many Hollywood couples who have distanced themselves form this continuous polygamy or polyandry. And if the unhappy, provocative, and delicious Marilyn Monroe, an abandoned daughter, hungry adolescent, and unadapted wife, was American, the English Elizabeth Taylor was a lovable and well-loved daughter. The love affairs of certain millionaires like Tommy Manville, king of asbestos, are always headline news; his vast fortune allows him to purchase the charms of wife after wife, some of whom haven't even been able to stick with him for more than twenty four hours, and to pay them substantial amounts of alimony upon their divorce. On the other hand, a certain millionairess has been able to pay for the luxury of having princes, adventurers, playboys and famous actors for husbands. Other powerful families, such as the DuPonts and the Rockefellers, have remained faithful to the puritan tradition of austerity. As happens everywhere, marriage and divorce are often no more than an act in American life as a whole, even though sexual pressure is far more intense and open than in France–in theory the Mecca for the libertine way of life. But even here, America shows its Puritanism–turned inside out.

Prostitution, which is common in the South and in the poorest and most wretched urban neighborhoods, is illegal and does not enjoy the same facilities as in Europe, even though both here and there, it is tolerated or covered up by the authorities. It is possible that it has become less viable on the one hand because of the freedom with which young people can meet and early marriage, both of which relieve pressure, and on the other, because of a certain respect for the role of women and puritanical prejudices. But periods of war intensify it. It is controlled by racketeers and gangsters like "Lucky" Luciano, whose recent (1961) funeral in his native Italy was as grand as that of a prince or duke from a bygone age. Police in the cities are reasonably tolerant. But from time to time we read about a raid on a hotel known to the police or on a "house of ill fame", as a result of which a number of women are arrested along with one or two respectable gentlemen of means from good families. News of the incident is quickly covered up or forgotten. The wife of a diplomat serving in the Middle East was arrested one night in a high-class brothel, which the police raided possibly because the madam had stopped paying her monthly "protection" fee; there was evidence that the elegant lady was charging one hundred dollars (the equivalent of two hundred nowadays, or six thousand escudos) for a few hours of jovial company. "It's my pin money!" explained the wandering diplomat's Penelope. (More recently, a one-time "madame", or pimp, published her memoirs about her profitable business–*A House is not a Home*–in which she recounted picturesque episodes and named politicians, millionaires who helped her make a living, and gangsters who exploited her. Born in the ghettos of Russia, she died not long ago in California, loved by men and by God. Moral scruples have never forbidden such confessions, which invariably cause a sensation and make a lot of money.) Psychiatrists publish serious, academic studies on *call-girls* and their problems. One thing is certain, especially since the publication of the famous Kinsey Reports: frigidity is a phenomenon of alarming proportions (as is also that of homosexuality), and social research indicates that poverty and crime are far from being the only or even major factors in prostitution.

Abundance of resources creates apparently benign, insidious forms of prostitution. Marriage followed shortly afterwards by a divorce settlement of prodigious proportions; an eventual short-lived union between an ambitious employee, star struck or without prospects, with her wealthy boss; the exhibition for commercial purposes of female charms in the theater, nightclub, magazines and advertisements–all wrapped up in a more or less disguised form of venality. Some businessmen hire the services of *call-girls* to entertain their important clients from overseas. The rule is always "make them happy." At so-called *stag-parties*, or social get-togethers exclusively for men, there are often girls present to excite their senses with striptease, belly dancing or dances of the seven veils, all for the greater glory of Business. As in so many other countries, there are often close links between the worlds of crime, politics, business, and even justice. A distinguished South American, inveterate admirer of the fair sex, tells me that a high-ranking conservative figure, who played a major part in the Politics of Good Neighborliness, maintained a virtual seraglio for the enjoyment of his most important visitors–a kindness to which our Latin American brothers are particularly susceptible.

Generally speaking, foreigners or outsiders come to understand certain aspects of the life of a great city that remain invisible to its residents, who are more given to routine. A visiting journalist told me that in the "family" hotel in the middle of Manhattan where he stayed, the bartender would recommend to him the services of girls who frequented the bar. The impassive black elevator attendant at the back of the building would take the guest and his companion to the relevant floor, without so much as a word. This same journalist told me how easy it was to get a girl anywhere in this country. Upon arriving at a hotel in Reno or Las Vegas, Nevada, a young *groom* asked him if he wanted some nice company for the night: "Yes, but let me see her first." The boy pushed through the crowd in the foyer, stopped behind a tall, blond beauty, and pointed to her discreetly. The deal was done–"and it wasn't at all expensive!" My interlocutor concluded.

Women dispose of a freedom that no one contests and even get rich by showing off their physical charms. The artistic director of one of the largest publishing houses in New York showed me some astonishing collections of photographs of girls used for modeling clothes (especially underwear), for advertisements inside and on the covers of magazines and the like. They are generally beautiful and very well paid–from forty to eighty dollars, and more, per hour's work–and, of course, they agree to every artistic whim of the photographer or director. But this line of work is strictly limited to girls between eighteen and twenty-two years of age. In order to "keep their figure" and their youthful freshness, these girls subject themselves to going hungry. Some even faint during the long hard sessions spent posing. Their ambition is to get into films or marry a rich man. How many dancers and chorus girls from the Ziegfeld Follies have married millionaires! The Powers Agency, in New York, is famous for recruiting beauties to become models. A tycoon set up one of these agencies so that he could get to know some girls; he ended up marrying one of them and tried in vain to turn her into a film star. All this cost him a fortune–and a turbulent divorce… Beauty pays, and it's legitimate business. The predominant presence in the popular crime, sex, and scandal press is that of the female, for whom terms of a peculiar vulgarity have been coined, such as *juicy blonde* and *burning brunette*… But the press in Latin America isn't far behind!"

A French restaurateur was explaining to a group of rich Latin Americans what love meant in the United States: "Look at the fruit in that fruit dish; they're beautiful, shiny, appetizing, aren't they? They have no taste whatsoever. They're like American women…" (Would it be correct for us to assume they're "green"?) A young woman companion of a Brazilian friend of mine, who complained about the coldness of "gringo" women and the insipidness of North American cuisine, told him one day: "Whew! You want to enjoy everything, even the food!

It happened in the 1930s. Mr. Appelgate, a respectable suburban dweller, poisoned his wife, with the complicity of his lover, a next-door neighbor, whose seventeen-year old daughter both he and she had also corrupted. The court sentenced them to death, and the husband of the poisoner tearfully insisted loud and clear that the adulteress was innocent and of good character, and publicly swore his undying love to her and grief at her passing… The depraved daughter told about the intimate scenes in which she had taken part; she showed the photographers her legs, and smiled flirtatiously… Innocent as she was, she received hundreds of marriage proposals and got herself a rich husband. Experience is an investment! The solemnity of the occasion reached its peak when veterans of the Great War paid military honors to their comrade who had been condemned to death.

In fact there's nothing easier, one could even say it's too easy, than to open a Hearst newspaper every day, or another one of the so-called "yellow press", to get a picturesque and partial view of American life, for that too produces a profit.

America has everything: Puritanism and debauchery, sadistic cruelty and unlimited gentility, generosity alongside an implacable hunger for money and lucre, instances of abject subjugation and single-minded independence. There is the *souteneur* and the faithful husband, the cold-hearted woman who sells her charms for millions without ever knowing happiness, and the sensitive and sensual woman who is not selfish in giving her love; the dissatisfied lesbian and the dried up virgin, the procuress and the pure young bride, the chaste young man and the brutal rapist, the husband who sues his wife's lover for "usurping her affections", the suicidal lover, the little street gypsy girl who invites the passer-by to visit her sister, the fortuneteller behind a curtain of cheap, stained cotton… There is something of everything, something of everything. But God help us if we try and judge, if we cast the first stone from inside our glass houses…

The problem of love lies essentially in the dignity of relations between the sexes. When I see women fulfilling efficiently and unselfishly many of the functions that were formerly the preserve of men, participating in all the demonstrations of intelligence and progress, or writing a high proportion of the books that get published–without forfeiting any of the charm, dignity or gentleness of their "feminine" role–I feel inclined to believe that we have taken a great step forward, even when, in their attempts to become the equal of men in society, they have acquired many of their vices. The conquest of human freedoms cannot be accomplished by misunderstandings or through the "war" of the sexes, nor by presuming that one party has total superiority over the other, but in loyalty, in the acceptance of common responsibilities, and in the joyous sharing of suffering.

All this induces my friend from Zacatecas to lament his fate at every turn: "Oh! What a paradise America is for women! They're the bosses here…" A free, responsible and self-sufficient woman, the woman he would wish to dominate and exploit, and cannot, makes him feel sick and gives him sleepless nights. He is married to an American woman from a "good family", and I suspect she makes him do the washing-up– supreme humiliation for any *Hombre!*–and maybe even throws his clothes at him… Our ideas and opinions are often merely the rationalization of our feelings, our humiliations, our stifled desires and impulses. The fact is that when he was six years old, he didn't walk round Zacatecas (or was it Tamáulipas?) hand in hand with his little girlfriend from school!

The Arrival

The decisive step across the line that divided the course of his past life from his future was when he boarded ship at Southampton on 4th July (1935), Independence Day, and therefore one of celebration for the more than one thousand passengers of all sexes–especially the opulent variety–who were assembled there to return to their country. Anchored offshore because there wasn't a long enough quay to accommodate it, was the *Normandie*, glowing with lights and promises. It was on its second voyage. The noise made by the mostly drunken crowd was deafening–roars, cries, acclamations, greetings, all the hurly-burly of some great event, as if the prospect of returning to the puritanical monotony of the business world were inducing in them one last outburst of unbridled excitement. The dresses, which were the last word in fashion, furs (in spite of the fact that it was summer), jewelry, perfumes (which had come from Paris along with their users), heavy make-up, the showy behavior, were (as he would only realize years later) the same as those of the pampered audiences on the opening nights at the opera or ballet and reflected the abusive freedoms of a society depicted by Hemingway and Scott Fitzgerald; so contagious was it that it even influenced the collective dreams of boundless freedom held by the emigrants lost among that multitude. No one there recalled the fatal voyages of the *Titanic* or the *Lusitania*, the maritime tragedies of the

First World War, nor did it occur to them how near they were to a second war–a mere four years away! A special launch was now about to transport all that seething community out to the Floating City that awaited them, its vast doors wide open, pouring its golden lights out into the darkness of the night and the waves. As for the stewards, tall, smiling, impeccable, dressed in tunics as if members of the Academy, they greeted that dollar-toting horde, guiding its individual components to their respective classes and cabins, or to the limitless facilities of that vast, sumptuous liner where the orgy was destined to continue for another four days and nights, in a dazzling atmosphere of luxury, art, taste, and order.

His own anxieties seemed to fade as a result.

*   *   *

And so one day, at last, he was able to smile at the distant memory of his arrival, when the City, bustling and brimming with mystery, surprised him for the first time. His only two friends there were waiting for him, one at each end of the huge arrivals hangar on the quay, now bathed in dusk and even nightfall, where the *Normandie* had tied up to unload its fifteen hundred passengers. What an emotional meeting! There were no difficulties whatsoever. Once the traveler's suitcase had been dispatched amid the uproar–two or three books, a dictionary, some papers and the bare minimum necessary of clothes (he was wearing his only suit and his one pair of shoes, both new)–they took him to have dinner at a restaurant on Eighth Street, in the Village. The place, the old-fashioned dining room, the select looking clientele, the hushed conversations, the laughter, the rear patio where they sat down under an awning, between the smell of cooking and summer vegetation, the red-jacketed waiters, tall, jet black, impassive, with just a slight air of disdain–everything seemed sumptuous to him and left him with the voluptuous impression of having arrived in an exotic, tropical country, in a word a colonial environment; the atmosphere was straight out of some English novel. And above all, the unexpected and surprising feeling of freedom, the ability to take a deep breath without having to explain yourself to anyone. He felt like taking his jacket off; looking around, however, he didn't dare. It was too soon; this would come some days later, at the counter of a *fish-and-chips* bar.

Afterwards, the modest apartment in a narrow, ordinary street, unpretentious and hidden away, welcoming like some home out of a dream or a love-nest that his dear friend had managed to conjure up (God knows at what price), and where she welcomed him with open arms–"Your home!"–so that he could start his life over again on another footing, with other influences and another destiny… He felt light-headed with a hope and a happiness that he had never felt before. Would he now, in the name of Love, be able to forget everything, bear everything, including jealousy? The friend lived out of town and, cordial and discreet, drove off in his car without delay, leaving them to themselves. Not alone, because there were two of them and they were together, although at last united in one being, in the heat of a renewed, passionate love, and because Love was a third and welcome presence and source of company, which embraced and enveloped them.

They went straight to bed and made love until they were exhausted, with all the hunger, the ardor, the laughter and tears of their brief meeting in Lisbon some months before, but now in the almost complete certainty that they would never be separated again. At the break of day, once the initial, urgent obligations of their passion had been satisfied, and (in his case) of his negligence and rapture, in order to show her his gratitude and to make her happy in this new sub-matrimonial state, which he in fact had never expected, he leapt out of bed: "I'll go and make some coffee and bring it to you in bed!" (How he wanted to spoil her!) But she replied: "God help you! It's very complicated and I'm not used to it." (Neither am I!) But why? First, there was the orange juice, then the egg had to be boiled for exactly the right time, watch in hand; the coffee wasn't like in Lisbon, in a bag, but filtered, he didn't know how much of the thickly ground coffee to use, and the water had to be *furiously boiling*! Good Heavens! As for milk, she never took it unless as a last resort; a touch of cream or evaporated milk was enough. (What on earth is *evaporated* milk?!) By that time the milk must have been delivered at the door, with its top of thick cream in the neck of the (almost) liter bottle. No, wait a minute! Someone–her sister in all probability–had put it in the *ice-box*. Another novelty: this was a type of small oak cupboard, with a compartment inside, a primitive refrigerator where a huge block of ice, which a man delivered every other day, would be placed ("Ice!"), and which (the box) would require all his attention; one careless moment, and the ice, having melted in the bowl or tray, would flood the kitchen–the main room at the entrance to the flat–inducing heated protests from the neighbor below, who was in charge of the building. "Ah! And the toast! Do you know how the electric toaster works?" He felt ashamed at being unable to handle so many technological wonders, but there was nothing to be done about it; he was in America, the land that was their home! She had told him during her short visit to Lisbon: "You've been warned; if one day you go to America, for a visit or to stay, you're forbidden to enter the kitchen!" (All very well, but it was he who had to fry her two eggs! And he had a feeling that he would soon be ready to become a *chef.*)

All this had given him food for thought: was he not by any chance seeking to exert over this independent woman his paternalistic, protectionist tendencies, which were his surreptitious way of imposing his male authority? She might begin to resent him too, like the other one had! Sure enough, some days later, while he was cutting his toenails with the ancient pair of scissors inherited from his late father (Lord! He'd been gone nine years already, and what with the dictatorship!), he found a new term of comparison: Men and women are like the big toes on a pair of feet: exactly the same but *opposite!* Or then again, like the image in a mirror: identical, but the other way round! What a great novelty! But it was precisely this that made Love so delicious and full of possibility, albeit complicated. He was delighted with this discovery, which would solve many a future problem. It was actually the first thing that exile taught him. By way of celebration, he went to the kitchen cupboard, where he had found the remains of a bottle of sweet Vermouth, and he drank a glass of it with crushed ice–how delicious it was in such hot weather! He hadn't had it since Madrid, eleven years before. (Ah! How he missed the Carrera San Jerónimo! (1924). And the Hotel Lisboa, and Maruja, pale and blond, in her grief!).

First thing that morning, after she had left, while shaving in front of the mirror in the bathroom (no longer would he be short of razor blades, although the humid climate would make them go rusty too), seeing the drops of sweat streaming down from his forehead and temples onto his face, he burst out laughing; he had never seen himself sweating! It reminded him of his father, with the ritual of kissing him on the cheek or the hand that so disgusted his children. He was astonished by the equatorial heat at such a northerly latitude. (Just wait until the winter and then you'll see!) The sultriness of July, aggravated by the almost suffocating humidity, made it imperative that one should take a bath or a shower every day, and sometimes twice daily. The steam from the shower formed condensation, which soaked the walls and tiles like a Turkish bath or sauna. The vigorous calisthenics of Love made them sweat even more, viscous, glutinous, their bodies stuck together! How they laughed (and bathed)! But of course it didn't make them stop. They made love at any hour they could, day or night, at sunrise and sunset, obsessively and repeatedly, with a fury that was almost vengeful in its determination to make up for lost time. Desperate love was his refuge against loneliness, uncertainty, and problems, as well as the intense focus upon those seven wasted years. He could hardly believe the suffering he had been through during those recent times. If it hadn't been for her, what would have become of him? She had rescued him from madness and maybe even suicide. That was why he loved her doubly, as if they had resumed a life they had been dreaming about since 1928. They were trying to eliminate the time in between. It was she he had loved first. Since then, everything had been an eternity measured in terms of disappointments, privations, sudden alarm, and disillusion.

For some time, he still felt the violent shuddering of the *Normandie*'s stern, a sort of counterpoint to the vibration of his nerves, which woke him up suddenly with a fright, as he imagined himself still aboard ship. The metal springs and mesh of the bed squeaked in chords of unusual musical harmony, accompanying the frenetic rhythm of Love. In fact it was not a bed but a *couch* (pronounced *cautche*) or a folding divan; the lower half could be stowed away during the day under the other. (When will we get a real bed?) One morning, in the early hours, he fell off the divan, as if shaken by some earth tremor; and indeed, according to the papers, there had been one: in Brooklyn, on the other side of the East River. The damage had been limited to some cracks in one or two decrepit walls.

Not everything was therefore easy or pleasurable. The contrast with his former life was huge, deprived as it had been. He came from the City supposedly of sunlight and moonlight, of vast suburban horizons, of clean, healthy air, as yet free of industrial fumes and dust; yes, indeed, but it was where he had even suffered hunger and other privations, devoured by blood-sucking mosquitoes, and where he used to take a bath in the clothes tub, and there he was suddenly a free prisoner of an area full of scrapyards! Immediately to the rear and side of that ground-floor apartment, there was a yard and a shed where there were piles of spare parts from worn-out cars, towers of tires and a thousand other articles for scrap lying around in a mess, as if the result of an earthquake. When he opened the window, the hot air would waft in, loaded with metallic particles, greasy, acidic exhalations, coal-dust and detritus and suffocating fumes. Ten times a day, he would clean the (wobbly) top of his desk, which became covered with a grainy film of dirt, and he would wash his hands another ten times. He even began to fear he had developed an obsession for order and cleanliness! That was how he described things in humorous letters to two or three friends back in Lisbon, in which he spoke of his solitude, his work, surroundings, the customs and habits he observed, his projects, but out of discretion and prudence, he never mentioned Love.

Everything was naturally strange to him, although new and the scene of his epic tale of love. He was stifled between flaking walls encrusted with salts, repainted a thousand times, with the creaky, uneven floor, the color of bull's blood or even black, with the head of nails sticking out of it, like in the ancient Pombaline houses of his childhood; when he washed it with great buckets of soapy water and a scrubbing brush, it let off a bitter smell of old age, of layers of paint and strata of dirt, of dampness and cat pee. The chemical cleaning fluids affected him (he had a sensitive nose!): "It's so clean it even stinks!" he concluded, laughing, and feeling like crying. "Oh! Sweet smells of Nature, where are you?" When would he be able to write again? For he found all this stimulating. It was all happening here in the world-famous Greenwich Village. There was no shortage of subject material. He must adapt. He had to. It was essential. Love, which lights up and transforms everything–*Che muove'l Sol e l'altre stelle!*–was transforming the *ghetto* into Paradise.

He stayed there the whole day, fired with gratitude, impatience, and desire. She would arrive home in the late afternoon, calm and smiling (Mona Lisa's smile!), and they would hurl themselves down the chasms of passion. Then she would sit down in front of her portable Remington (so many papers to see to!), straight-backed in her lace dress over a fiery orange background, and he, seated on a stool by her side, gazed at her in adoration from top to bottom; she tapped away swiftly at the keyboard. Ever smiling, biting the inside of her cheeks, a habit she never lost. From down below in the basement, where the *janitor* (from the Latin, Jano, an archaic touch to describe the caretaker) lived with his wife or a girl-friend, there rose the muffled sounds from a radio at that hour, the voice of a *torch-singer* (Helen Morgan no doubt), solemn and dramatic, the sensual and provocative mystery of *night-club* tunes: a strange, seductive world! He liked all that, found it inspiring, vaguely anticipating he knew not what: something that would certainly never be! Other times, there were arguments: the man was reputed to be a former gangster! All this excited him and helped him to set the scene, to make it credible.

Or they would have visitors, her younger sister almost every day; she was a decorator and puppet maker, an angel, or there were the two lesbians, delightful girls, well-dressed, very feminine–nothing like that awful butch, Gertrude Stein! Sometimes groups of them would turn up and fill him with indefinable yearnings. Two of them, sitting either side of him on the divan one afternoon, began to admire his chestnut-colored shoes, which had been specially made by a cobbler who worked at the bottom of a staircase in a doorway at Intendente, for a mere eighty (yes, 80!) escudos, and were indeed a fine piece of Portuguese artwork. Nor could they believe it: what a trifle! Flattered, was he already dreaming of converting them? (Some of them cut both ways in their love lives.) A frequent visitor was B, a Chilean friend and neighbor, an architect's assistant, who one afternoon brought him a surprise, just imagine! The general secretary of the Communist Party! A ginger-haired Irishman by the name of Hathaway, a typical laborer or seaman in build, a "blue-collar worker", who spoke heatedly like a former anarchist who had been converted to the new cause. He even reminded him of Bento Gonçalves! (It wasn't long before he was replaced by a man of superior mental capacity, and he never again heard of the affable and talkative Hathaway, who at least had had the curiosity to come and meet a Portuguese "comrade" in exile!)

Although he could express himself with relative ease in English, he found it difficult to understand the average American behind a counter or at a ticket office; if he couldn't catch what was being said and repeated his question, they would become impatient and give him a distorted answer. They were Europeans like him but without the veneer of patience and would leave him disconsolate. He could understand the Jews much better, for they were skilled in expressing themselves (the educated ones), people like Minna, a warm, gentle woman, a good friend and lawyer, who pronounced each syllable clearly: "Are you working hard?" Not a consonant was lost! Or did she do it on purpose so that he would understand her better? Then one night, she took them to meet a young couple she knew who were also Jews, he a law professor at New York University, and she one of the prettiest women he had ever met or would ever meet in his life: the type with very dark eyes that contrasted with the radiant whiteness of her skin, passionate and fiery, as if they were deliciously lubricated–if you see what I mean! The husband was a Trotskyite. They had the most lively of discussions, he (taking the position of a Stalinist), with his still rudimentary English, had the last word, while the wife backed him, and seemed to be devouring him with those unforgettable eyes, while he all but fell in love with her. The professor was ashamed, and jealous as hell! They never saw each other again. It was common in that country. In those days, thanks to his Marxist reading, everything seemed clear and straightforward to him. Even the question of how to appeal to the opposite sex!

With B and his friend, Myrtila, who was a sculptor, they took some photos in the dark, damp, silent inner-courtyard of the building, with its almost total lack of greenery. The dark-skinned Estela, sweet and languid, had a gently happy expression, with her Giaconda's smile! He, in his well-cut gray suit for all seasons, the work of a modest tailor in the Rua dos Fanqueiros, was unusually elegant!

When he was at home alone and someone knocked on the door or the telephone rang, he never answered it: for the sake of caution and out of fear of not understanding. One afternoon, he took no notice of the doorbell, and before long he got a fright when he heard a great commotion in the bathroom; someone was trying to get in through the window, which was always open, and shouting back to someone outside! They were either burglars or the police! He ran to see; it was his future brother-in-law, the youngest one, who was eighteen years old: "Joe! You didn't answer so we thought there was no one at home! Sorry!" He couldn't believe that someone might enter peoples' houses through the bathroom window, but still!… That was freedom! They laughed. The lad was delivering some household goods that they needed.

Sometimes he had the uncanny but happy feeling that life would continue like that indefinitely, humble, anonymous, safe, without great ups or downs, and tinged with Love: his dream! He was happy in his obscurity, far from documents and formalities, which he had always hated, just any old Tom, Dick or Harry. He didn't depend on anyone–wishful thinking that would soon be proved wrong! He just thought it a pity there were no Redskins around! His American education had been limited to the works of Gabriel Ferry, Mayne Reid and Gustave Aimard, in novels about Red Indians ("rojos" in Spanish), Texas-Jack, less so Buffalo Bill, in the crime stories of Nick Carter, Miss Boston, Nat Pinkerton, Patrick Osborn, full of racism and hostility towards the workers (which he hated!), and even in the work of a Portuguese consul, which had gripped him but he had forgotten the author's name! And finally, the short stories and some poems by Edgar Poe! The only author he didn't read (among those who wrote about Indians) was Fenimore Cooper. Much later he would come to read De Tocqueville, and then, after he had finished his university studies, D. Pasquet's book–*The Political and Social History of the American People* (1924), an extraordinary work by a Frenchman! And others, such as *Amerika*, by an innocent sixteen-year-old Kafka, in which the Statue of Liberty is described as brandishing a

Roman sword rather than a bow and arrow! It was more reminiscent of the (bad) pamphlets by Nick Carter. So that was what America was for him: *This is America for me* (in the words of the song). Of course, with the passage of time, he would read hosts of North American historians, but it would require many pages to mention them all!

He was as poor as ever and even more so. It wasn't that he was starving, for she had a modestly paid job, there were the translations, and he would no doubt find an occupation; there were films to be translated (just imagine!), and there were Brazilian friends... As for the Portuguese, they gave him no cause for hope! He didn't even present himself at the Consulate. It took a former colleague of his, now vice-consul, to visit him: "So you've been here for two weeks, and not so much as a whisper?!" But he was a political exile!... It would have to wait.

At least he could now put his hand in his pocket and feel a few coppers, not many, but enough for a newspaper, cigarettes, coffee, and even a couple of cinema tickets. He had her to thank. Dear woman! Unfortunately, as a temporary "visitor", he was prohibited from taking paid employment. So how were they going to live?! That was a serious problem. And then there was the danger of the "blue laws": the sacred commandments of puritan morality–no adultery, living in sin, promiscuity... (But *de facto* marriage between cohabiting couples was allowed by *common law*). On the other hand, prostitution flourished before their very eyes; it was illegal, of course. In the hands of Mafiosi. Even Gorky himself had been invited to leave the country because he had arrived in the company of his "lady friend"! This, in spite of the fact that they slept in different rooms, in the same luxury hotel. Corruption is permeated with such hypocrisy–or could it be the other way round?

They discussed the matter anxiously. As he was still married to the Other, wasn't there a risk that this woman might come and catch them in their current state? There certainly was, that was true. Apparently, she even had relatives in Yonkers, a town not far away. He might be arrested or expelled! Well, that was obvious... "When all is said and done, I didn't come under the understanding that we would live together, did I?" (But how else was he to survive?) Estela looked at him with solemn concentration. How stupid and thoughtless of him to say such a thing! Feeling that nothing could separate them now. How could she put up with such an insult? "Only for the sake of appearances..." he added, making matters worse. For here, there are no "appearances"! Very well then, and with her usual imperturbable serenity and self-control, she began to help him look for another apartment in the same building or next door, where he could live alone. What a silly idea! Where would they find the money for more rent? They gave up, of course.

He was pursued by memories of the Other Woman and had feelings of remorse. Could it be that he had abandoned her without due reason? Had he dispatched her in a moment of blind impulse? But then hadn't she been to blame for wrecking all his plans and dreams? He would have to write a novel about it… Maybe one day! The contrast between these two women was striking. Could it be that he had made a mistake in his choice? Which one? Both had inspired his love in their different ways. Only a few days after he had arrived, a card had come for him: "I'm in Lisbon waiting for you." So much for that! Foolish or malicious friends had given her his address, contradicting what had been agreed. What could he do? He didn't answer. But the nagging doubt over the suddenness of his decision or choice remained.

The past he had tried to break with—both his and that of his women—was therefore not dead and buried, as he had supposed when he had dug an Atlantic trench to separate both halves of his life. Here she was coming to disturb and torment him in the midst of his freedom and supposed happiness! As he failed to show up, she soon went back to her country of origin. That was when he began to get letters from female friends and cousins; he hesitated to open them. "Magda's short of food!" "To go on studying she's having to work as a waitress in the students' canteen and put up with insults…" With all that, he found it hard to swallow his meager lamb chop at lunch, as he thought about what she was going through. If only he could change his status from visitor to immigrant and earn some money! (Doing what?) But it was complicated, if not impossible, and an expensive business. He would have to hire an attorney. He was overcome once more by anguish. Could it be that Estela was aware of it? He didn't dare talk to her about the matter. He was playing a game of ambiguity and dissimulation; in a vague attempt to get even with her (out of jealousy for her past!), he slyly began to engage in a sort of undercover correspondence with the Other Woman! After all they had the memory of a past together. It was a blatant piece of infidelity, and remorse piled up doubly upon remorse. But perhaps he found such dramatic situations interesting. He had been born for them! As for going back to the past, perish the thought! And shouldn't she be jealous of him too?! His marriage had been a real betrayal of implicit promises (that is, promises that had never been openly stated). In her impassiveness, she never gave any sign of such feeling. This only increased his doubts; didn't she really love him? How is it possible to love someone and *not feel jealous?!* Or didn't she love him with the same degree of passion that he devoted to her? Yes, for sure, because he could now see that he had never loved any other woman so deeply!

He couldn't suggest bigamy to her, a *ménage-à-trois!* Very well, then, she would make the ultimate sacrifice by encouraging her rival to come over! What a suggestion! Such an absurd idea didn't bear thinking about. Was it her calmness, her sense of *fair-play*, perhaps her perpetual serenity masking passion? Her unfathomable sensuality, satisfied without a commitment to love?... And at this point, her indulgence only made his jealousy worse. It was a vicious circle! That was when the Other Woman–how cunning people can be!–dissimulating, sneaky, imagining herself to be irreplaceable and the victor, claimed that her former biology professor, whose name escapes me, who had expressed such an interest in her after her first-year exams, was now providing her with "vital support", was being a "great help", and that she didn't want to "offend" him! To kill off his illusions maybe? *The poor little wretch!!* What a nerve she had! It had to be seen to be believed. Threats and blackmail were the last straw–but in her extreme astuteness, she resolved the problem for him; he expelled her from his flesh and his thoughts. Let her look after herself. *I'm having a hard time here too!* (Was he exaggerating? Maybe not after all.) And he halted his secret adulterous correspondence with his wife.

But he was now going to learn that Life, like coins, always has two sides: heads and tails!

*   *   *

Indeed, there was the problem of retrospective jealousy, which had not yet been resolved. There was the episode of the kitten, for example! They had called her *Bendéry*, by strange coincidence, the name of a port in the country of the Other Woman's birth, and which had been annexed from Romania ever since the First World War. Why? Because this–and this was total torment to him–was also the name of the French steamship on which she had traveled from New York to Lisbon and back, on that second and unforgettable journey she had made in 1932, to see for herself his rumored marriage to the "Russian woman" (who wasn't in fact Russian).

On the afternoon she left, she had invited him on board and introduced him to a taciturn looking officer (the purser?) who had offered him a *drink* and looked at him with the fixed expression of someone who was suspicious of his motives or a rival–in fact, the feeling was mutual! He hadn't liked the fellow at all. Was it out of instinct? What was the invitation for? Was it deliberate, in order to vex him? To show him that he wasn't the only man in the world? And now, here was a kitten, only a few weeks old, *a present from that very same gentleman*, or named with him in mind, to prove that, TWO OR THREE YEARS AFTER THAT VOYAGE, she still continued to see the sailor, maybe in this very house! (Or no, because before he arrived, she lived in a Residence only for women.) But in any case, frequenting the same Village circles, which were hers too! Was any further proof needed?... This confirmed his suspicions about her hateful liaison. And then again there was the story of the three-day trip to Spain, supposedly to visit her three aunts in Cadiz. Couldn't she do it in one? How many did she need?...

His jealousy overflowed into anger and reproach: didn't she realize all this showed her up and gave the game away in the matter of the cat? And wasn't it distressing for him? Hadn't she thought about the effect this could have on their relationship? (Or had she done it on purpose?) Might she be–but he never dared say this to her!–one of those good-time girls, more often than not Americans, well-known throughout the world and the subject of saucy tales among men who worked on the sea or in tourism? (And as for Paris, *oh-lá-lá, les Americaines*!) A pilot friend of his had told him one day: "Once these broads step onto the deck of a ship, they lose any sense of shame or dignity and throw themselves at the first man in a crisp white uniform with braids, with whom they dance a *fox* or a *shimmy*, and who flatters their vanity!" Both sides indulging in tourist prostitution on the high seas! With this thought, he burst out angrily: "Why didn't you at least get rid of the cat before I arrived?! Or do you think I have no memory?"

And that's what she did right away, prudently, and without any comment: the crucial evidence in the body of a poor creature who wasn't to blame for any of these symbolic concerns or rumors! As for the sailor, he never again (as far as he knew) showed his face in or around the house. Wasn't it obvious? *He'd been warned*! But then couldn't a woman show a man friendship or gratitude, without straightaway arousing suspicion...? Well, you can't fool me! But who knows? All her past seemed to him to be tainted, even before their distant first meeting in 1928.

Once his torture had begun, it grew, swelled up, proliferated. Everything now became a cause for jealousy. Obsessed and somewhat dishonestly, when she was out, he furtively studied her American passport, the same one she had had three years before, so as to check the dates, especially those relating to the mysterious and unexplained three-day visit to Spain, on the blind impulse, he suspected, of seeking revenge on him for having discovered he had got married: *the dates fitted!* And that was surely not the first encounter with the anonymous subject (or object?) of what was clearly–what? A romantic trip? Well, what else could it have been?! They must already have known each other: where and how? During those years of his innocence or inexperience, hadn't she written to him one day, on a photo of herself she had sent him, in which another figure had been cut out: *"Are you jealous?"* How young they are when they learn these things and how clever they are!

He felt betrayed, made to look a fool, the victim of a trap. So what should he do now? Uncontrollable, brandishing her passport–the proof!– he forced her to confess to her irreparable waywardness, a scar that would mark them forever. He was so livid that he could have killed someone. Caught in the clutches of his own contradictions, he interrogated her yet more harshly. He now insisted on knowing–suffering!–more: who, when, where, how? Like another version of Dostoyevsky's *Eternal Husband*... She, terrified but calm, answered him as if addressing someone who was insane; no doubt unaware amid all this of any misdemeanor worthy of censure or punishment; the clarity of her conscience left him exasperated, as if it were a manifestation of "Anglo-Saxon cynicism", or perhaps because it suggested implicitly a charge that he was the real culprit of any deviance: for if he had got married, without any warning to her as an interested party, what did he deserve or what could he expect unless something of that sort?! (What? So one person's guilt justified that of another?! Two wrongs don't make a right!) With difficulty, he controlled his vindictive fury. But then one day, having forgotten his insulting comments, in the heat of a moment of passion, intimacy, and romantic satisfaction, she, grateful to him for his untiring attentions and wishing to praise him, confided candidly: "You're just like a man I had a six-month affair with!" He, placing his hand over her mouth (in order not to strangle her), shouted: "Not another word!"–and he withdrew from her abruptly... So that was it, was he going to last six months, in spite of his proven virile quality and technique, the object of passing enjoyment or the whim of an irresponsible adventure!? IS THAT WHAT LOVE WAS? And how many more had there been in the past? *In that case, what am I doing here? Who am I? What did I come here for?* He wanted to kill this unknown rival, *Portuguese* into the bargain–in other words, a boast and a show-off, who was alive and well somewhere, and who was having a good laugh at the expense of this innocent fool! His reaction was so obvious in both his behavior and expression, that she looked at him for the first time in genuine alarm under the immediate threat of repressed aggression. Was he another man? But then–he reflected–wasn't the comparison she made the highest praise to which he could aspire *as a man*? Notwithstanding, his bitterness remained, albeit silently.

One afternoon, Mr X, an elderly, respectable engineer, her former boss and (at least) on evidence no more than that unless a possible suitor, came to visit her, no doubt to see for himself the much younger rival who had won her. After the man had left, he made such a scene that for the first time she burst into tears and uttered her first cry of revolt: "That one, I love as a father! If he were to come back now, I would rush to give him a hug!" But was she thinking of the fatal consequences that such an act might have for both of them–*us*? And wouldn't that be tantamount to an invitation for them to separate? He realized the danger he was in… But (once again) how astute women were in creating situations that had no solution!

Other suspicions tormented him. He began to see "lovers" (former ones) in all her male acquaintances, whether there or elsewhere. Women are so easy! And what was he gaining from all this, he, in his obsessive insistence on monogamy? Did he want to lose her? Prove that she was unworthy of his love? Did he want to leave–to go where and to whom? Perhaps he derived some masochistic pleasure out of all this! (And who knows…) What next? Would he allow himself to go the full course to despair and suicide? After so much suffering? *All because of a woman!* He, who had sworn he would chop his balls off rather than submit to the whims of the Other Woman? (Poor girl!). Lord, what a place he had come to in search of Love! A den of puritanical innocence, or unconscious corruption? And if she were another Isadora Duncan, Lou Salomé, Frieda Van Richtophen (Lawrence's woman), or Alma Mahler, who belonged to the composer, and to Gropius, and to Werfel, and to Kokoshka, and God knows how many others?! In that order or another? What could he do about it, if he loved her? Would he take everything lying down, like all those other lovers who were so undemanding? Should he leave her? Would he suffer forever afterwards? Did he have to resign himself to realizing she was free?…Oh! That was too much!…

It was an insoluble problem. One of her female friends, who he had supposed was a lesbian, even went so far as to say: "Oh! He's delicious! So highly-strung! If you ever get sick of him, I'll take him on lease!" *Get sick of? Lease him?* Was this what the dreamt-of Village was all about?

Promiscuity, libertinism, the collectivization of sex, a trade in lovers? What had become of a world in which he had tried to remain pure, chaste, or loyal? (Had he tried? Or had he merely dreamt it?) No woman had ever made him feel so bad: not even Concha the prostitute, or the Lady from Rose Tree House, a bourgeois woman, married and with children, who had put him on a pedestal and from whom he had fled!... *And why did I run away? Lord Jesus–because I didn't love them!* That was the explanation, LOVE! And yet, possibly because of the influence of his present surroundings, it wasn't long before he himself began to feel tempted by the idea of erotic pluralism and dreamt of fixing himself up with other "women friends"... But with what means? Serial love brings with it obligations! Wasn't he becoming corrupted too? How did these men (and others too) allow themselves to fall for women who had known one or more lovers or husbands, showing a sensitivity which was comparable to that of so many other natural males?... They had always intrigued him; what pleasure, what freshness did they find in these women? *And didn't I leave the innocent Magda, whom I had supposedly idolized?* What is jealousy if not a neurosis about inferiority, the fear of supposing oneself to be negatively compared to, or confronted with, (an)other male(s)? Envy, scorn, the fear of intimate appearances? And wanting to kill them just for that! Might it not be that jealousy was hatred in disguise, its first manifestation? And yet, the dream of Woman's purity, that ancestral inheritance he suffered from!... *Fiddlesticks!*

So what was the point of tormenting this loving, saintly woman, who had made every effort to save him and win him back even second- or umpteenth-hand? Wasn't that what Love was? Why shouldn't there be mutual respect between them? What more could he ask for or expect at the age of thirty-four (and she thirty!)? As well as kindness, she possessed good faith and equanimity, a spirit of self-sacrifice and desire to do good, a sense of *fair-play*, compromise, and concord, individual freedom, a courage and common sense that seemed to contradict her supposedly libertine past! Perhaps that was the inevitable previous condition for the fervent love that he now enjoyed! He had been the slave of prejudice, of the prestigious privilege of Woman's virginity that had hypnotized him ever since childhood! Was he about to free himself once and for all? Or was it perhaps the visual beauty of an intact or little used sexual organ that fascinated him? Had not a friend of his of more than seventy years of age once said to him: "Is there any more beautiful thing in the world to contemplate?" A sort of *kosher* imbibed along with tradition? (But why had God endowed them with that tell-tale membrane?) For men are also the victims of cultural inheritance!

Yes, well everything was therefore a question of culture (or esthetics) rather than morality. Was it not a strange contradiction between a penchant for chastity and virtue, monogamy, fidelity, for which he had suffered so much (not without transgressing them occasionally)–and his current orgiastic impulses towards a type of bohemian promiscuity and "typological" variety? ("I love all women!...") Was he the victim of her influence? Or of his environment? What right did he have to expect a standard of virtue from her that he himself had violated and that he dreamt of breaking again?

He owed her (apart from love) the possibility of achieving the "great work" that he dreamt about and didn't yet know what it was. Gradually, he was seized by a sense of gratitude and admiration, a powerful feeling of tenderness and affection, which would enable him to live at peace with himself and to her contentment. He thought of the renowned Lou Salomé, and the many men she had perhaps belonged to, without their ever possessing her in spirit–and only with difficulty her body! He restrained any bitter feelings of jealousy as best he could, by attempting to rationalize it so as to free himself from it and be happy. For all the good things in life consist of giving and taking, as he was slowly beginning to learn with her.

Deep within him, however, in spite of his efforts and appearances, and though recognizing his own (involuntary) guilt, and legitimizing her past, he never achieved the super-human miracle of complete forgiveness. A dormant desire to get even remained within him, and sometimes came to the surface, and which he felt he had a right to given that he had suffered such a long period of monastic privation in his youth. This would lead him to fantasize and to occasional infidelities that would only cause them, and especially him, unwanted suffering.

Linoleum '36

These New York mornings, with their occasional placid provincial air, no longer know how to sing the song of silence: or they were born devoid of the power of learning. (Can it be that I am unable to hear it?) It is a Saturday of pale sunlight in Downtown; up above, the skyscrapers, which are empty today, recall the shell of some lost civilization, or underwater cliffs raised millennia ago by legions of sponges or foraminifers. The gleaming light towers seem to absorb the clarity of the sky and then spread it down here, onto the leprous old houses, in a fascinating contrast of grandeur and minuteness. Between the uniform, dirty brick façades, some of which are painted red and others white, up which worm-like fire escapes climb, festooned with rags and plants rendered colorless by lack of sunlight, the narrow streets, dating from the days of the Dutch, smell of toasted coffee, spices, and naval stores; they evoke a cosmopolitan emporium, like Lisbon in the age of the sailing ships and conquests. But everything is dark behind the dusty windows like sightless eyes. And to think that people live around here! In the oblique, absent sunlight, particles of metal, gasoline, and burnt coal glisten. We are breathing (I discover to my horror) a mineral laden air! There is a time-honored torpidity here, and the very impurity of the air has a certain Puritanism about it, the stillness of the Sabbath, a relaxed and all-embracing peace, an underlying voluptuousness. As I pass by, my eyes look down the side streets for the prows of the sailing clippers moored to the wharves, as in the old prints. (You can still see them in Brooklyn.) In the restaurants and gloomy cafés, with their filtered lights, their tarnished or engraved windows and their beveled mirrors of a now obsolete luxury (*Ladies Invited* Founded in 1872), sailors, bohemians, businessmen missing the hurly-burly of the weekdays, leaning on the bar, silent or exchanging laconic comments with each other, listen inattentively to the indolent, suburban voice of Bing Crosby or Rudy Vallee, the Tap dance of Fred Astaire, the baseball commentary–things that come from a future world. And then all of a sudden the whole scene seems like a residue of an age and a Europe that no longer exist; we sink into a gentle colonial torpor.

On the platform of a carriage dating from the 70s, a gentleman in a straw hat, an optimist, reads a Hearst newspaper with scrupulous care, as if it were the latest version of the New Testament. A black man, white from dirt and dust, a mole from deep in the bowels of a building site, weak with exhaustion, sleeps in a corner, his mouth wide open and dribbling, under the implacable infra-red rays. And the "Elevated" passes by, in the lethal silence of Saturday, between the silent impenetrable façades, like a roar of thunder on Judgment Day: screeches as it goes round curves, a grinding of brakes, a clattering of wheels, a groaning of metal and loose planks, clouds of brown dust. It's as if everything is going to collapse… At this point, we are plunged into an even louder, infernal racket; covered in metallic dust, their brows wrinkled and tense, their eyes dazed and jaws set, shaken by the vibration of their pneumatic drills, the men attack the steel girders as if they wanted to annihilate this confused, sluggish serpent that crawls and snakes its way along the length of Manhattan. A red flag… (What!? But it hasn't yet…) A strident whistle–and the explosive drills, the hissing, the abundant sweat, the shower of gold and blue sparks, all cease their offensive for a moment. These hardworking ghosts turn slowly, and we roll past carefully through the middle of the truce, and almost silently. Once again, there's a casual wave of the flag, the whistle pierces through the empty air, and the men return to their hostilities, spitting a thick, bitter, yellow phlegm.

How stimulating the City is! And I begin to love it…

Walking in the latticed shadow of the "El", down one of these empty streets, I suddenly feel as if something light and sticky has splattered on my shoulder, and I look: a huge lump of spittle full of chewed, liquefied peanut is oozing down my sleeve! Furious, I look upwards; on top of the metal structure, four or five floors above me, the train is slowing down as it enters a curve. His elbows on the rail of the platform, a black man smiles down at me mockingly, with a flash of his white teeth; he aimed his projectile at my head, and only missed his target by a couple of inches. I shake my fist at him impotently–a fat lot of good it will do me! The train disappears down the next street, as sinuous and narrow as a canyon. I go into a bar and make straight for the washroom to try and clean this gift. No dry-cleaners in the world will be able to remove such a stain!

A few days ago, K and I went to have a few beers at one of these grand old German restaurants in the area, to discuss our journalistic dreams; we had ambitious plans–to establish an information and news service, "the Something-or-Other Press", aimed at Latin America. As we left, evening was falling and the shadows from the "El" were lengthening on the sidewalk. We were walking along side by side, talking in a low tone, when two well-dressed young men approached us on the narrow sidewalk. I don't know what happened. No one spoke. It was like when two mastiffs that have never seen each other before, confront one another in the street and suddenly get entangled, growling and with their teeth bared. One of them advanced towards K, pointing two stiff, thick fingers towards his eyes. I stood stock still, more out of shock than fear (I would only feel this later). K leapt backwards with unexpected agility, pulled a flick-knife out of his back pocket, and standing firmly, shouted: *"Come on then, you bum!"* Four or five inches of steel glinted in the half-light. The other one had stopped short, and was about to launch himself forward again when his companion held him back from behind: "Leave him alone, lets go!" The assailant mumbled something, and we dodged past each other, while they continued on their way as if nothing had happened. Ashen-faced, K turned to watch them go, his knife open, then he snapped it shut, and put it back in his pocket. We walked on. I began to tremble. I couldn't understand why the man hadn't attacked me, seeing how skinny I am. I attract hostility! "What was all that about, then?" I asked. "Do you know him?" "I've never seen him before! He picked a quarrel with me. Did you see? He wanted to dig my eyes out! But he got the worst of it. I lived seven years in the Brazilian outback, selling drugs. I'm always on my guard!"

What hope, illusion or nostalgia still brings me here today? What am I looking for? K lived in one of these three-storey houses with three narrow windows on the front, nowadays squeezed between office blocks which house the millions made out of coffee and cacao[1]. He was a German by birth and Brazilian by adoption. It was only later that I heard he had a penchant for the *Herrenvolk* and was not well seen by the North

American authorities. He was arrested one day for disturbing the peace; one Sunday (having had a skinful the previous night), he went and stood in front of his window, huge, pink, and stark naked, to see if he could attract the attention of any possible female neighbors. There were complaints. A diplomat who was protecting him, saved him from embarrassment. With the outbreak of war, he decided to go back to Brazil on his motorcycle, crossing the entire continent from North to South. Did he ever get there? I had news of him from Guatemala. After that, silence.

I never got to know what happened to the articles I wrote about the abdication of Edward VIII of England–"I'm not a king, I'm a captive..."– the legacy of old man Rockefeller, and goodness knows what else. I even interviewed Cardinal Cerejeira, on board the Italian liner that was bringing him to New York. What I do know is that I never saw any money!

Note

[1] The whole of the picturesque area of Water Street, near Wall Street, has recently been demolished (1969). (Author's note.)

On a Visitor's Visa

In the dull silence of the room–there were two more separated from this one and from each other by large opaque glass partitions, with their doors always open–he typed the lunchtime translation on the unfamiliar machine with two hesitant fingers, and by the light of bulbs hanging from the ceiling, and in full glow in the middle of a snowy January morning. Opposite him, bent over the blue stencil, Don Silas de Sólis, with his shiny bald pate and eyeglass on its black cord, bemoaned each and every typing error under his breath–he called them *lapsus machinae* and would slap the lid of the pot of type-correcting fluid down on top of the table with an alarming clatter. "Why do you do that?" "So that he's aware that I made a mistake, and understands how much I suffer, as a slave!" "So why don't you go and tell him to his face?"

"He" operated in one of the compartments that had a window overlooking the street. In the other, the Irish secretary silently cut out articles from huge piles of newspapers that had arrived in sacks from Latin America. On hearing the voice of the boss–*"Señor Sólis, one moment!"*– the slave–*"Coming right away!"*–would jump up, rub the soles of his shoes repeatedly on the gray linoleum floor covering, and run doglike to his call. "Lackey!" his new young colleague sneered.

Once again there was silence, broken only by the rustling of newspapers, Don Silas, an inveterate smoker, clearing his throat, and the intermittent and sleepy tap- tapping of typewriters as they chewed the propaganda. The mixture of the smell of old newspapers, coupled with that of stale tobacco, and the accumulation of sweat and grease, made the overheated air even more stuffy. He took off his coat. He didn't go there out of any obligation, but because he still lacked friends or any other occupation in this huge, mysterious city, and the loneliness he felt at home was unbearable. "Do you mind if I come and do my translations here?" D. D. Martinson was delighted; this new translator was a university man and brought the firm prestige. (He had no other reward.) It was Don Silas de Sólis who did not welcome him with any goodwill; he was a rival, and Portuguese to boot! Is there anything worse than rivalry in slavery? All the more so because the new arrival detested this scissors and paste journalism and paid publicity, all written in the archaic, verbose Spanish of a former follower of Porfirio Diaz: oil concerns, large companies, international banks, and above all campaigns against the Mexican Government. Such was the Inter-American Press Service, better known overseas by its initials IAPS. ("And you as a Mexican, offer your services to this?") And as if that wasn't enough, miserably paid. But there wasn't anything else! Life as an expatriate was difficult enough, with all the problems he had brought with him and those he had left behind, unresolved; but this made him more bitter, corroded his joy in living, the novelty and excitement of his new surroundings. Oh! Freedom, what a high price you command!... Her love for him was his only refuge and consolation. But she went out to work all day and every day, and he at least had to earn some money for the rent (or not even that). The future looked bleak to him.

Five or six months before, in the excitement of arrival, with thirty dollars in his pocket, of the novelty of it all, and above all of love, everything had seemed welcoming, attractive and possible. But his visitor's visa, valid for six months, prohibited him from taking paid work. Even in order to obtain it, she had had to take out a loan in order to pay a warranty as his guarantor, and the interest on this was very high. What an angel she was. She and Mr. Martinson (he had a sharp eye did this aristocrat from Virginia!) had acted as his *sponsors* or patrons. It was a complicated country. And his situation was a delicate one; if he was caught working, he would be deported or invited to leave the country "voluntarily", at no expense to the Treasury. They would be expelling him, and he would be the one paying! Or would his sponsors be the ones left with the check? Deporting someone cost the State a fortune. But where would he go or return to? And what would he live on meanwhile? The illegal manual workers are the lucky ones, because they protect each other, go into hiding or change their abode, and go on working under an assumed name, and the Immigration Service sometimes doesn't even know of their existence! Unless they are betrayed to the authorities (almost always over a gambling matter, or a woman). But for "intellectuals"…

In order to gain time and negotiate his re-entry as an immigrant, on the advice of a lawyer, he had sent piles of documents and photocopies to the United States Consul in Toronto, Canada, and had requested an extension of his visa from the Immigration Service. He had already been summoned to Ellis Island, a sinister entrepôt for immigrants, in order to answer questions: Why had he come to the United States? Why did he want to stay? What was he living on and how much money did he have? Was he an anarchist? Or was he seeking to bring down American institutions by force?—He was a suspect as far as those functionaries were concerned, dressed in police-style uniforms, impenetrable behind their tribune-counter, which made the scene reminiscent of a court martial.

The door opened suddenly, and he looked up in alarm. A man came in, leaned against the door-frame staring hard at him, and directed a question to no one in particular: "Mr. D.D. Martinson?" (Hell! Where have I seen those green eyes before? That ruddy face, that tangled silver hair?) The nasal tones of the boss's voice, from inside (or outside): "That's me! What can I do for you?" He wanted to know the whereabouts of a certain (he looked at his paper) Portuguese by the name of J. Rolo, and what he was doing. (That must be me, yours truly thought, freezing momentarily). Mr. Martinson wanted to know who he was and why he was asking: "I'm from the Immigration Service. You were his sponsor, maybe you can give us some information." (Maybe?!) ("That's true, but he hasn't shown up round here. I don't even know whether he's still here. Perhaps you should ask Miss Alvarado.") He lifted the receiver. The officer didn't take his eyes off his victim, caught red-handed, contravening the Labor laws (or the laws of Idleness?), earning a pittance, sweating, feigning indifference, his fingers stumbling across the keyboard and making numerous errors, my God why can't the floor just swallow me up?

"Miss Alvarado? Good day, Martinson here. Do you know if Mr. Rolo is still here, or whether he's gone back to Portugal?" (…..) "Thank you." And he put the phone down. To the inspector: "She doesn't know either. I'm very sorry. Do you need anything else?" (The courage with which the fellow lies, with me right here, under the gaze of that hunting dog of a policeman, who seems to recognize me! But from where?) That was when he recognized him; he was the officer who had been a silent witness at his interrogation on Ellis Island! He felt as if he was actually sinking into the floor (but sadly, this wasn't so). And the man, who must have realized who he was, didn't say anything or ask any indiscreet questions!

"Okay, if he shows up round here, tell him we want to see him. It's urgent. My name's Inspector McGee." He shot a last flaming glance at the victim, said "Good afternoon", and left. It was obvious that he was absolutely furious. Mr. Martinson laughed cynically from inside his office, a nasal southern drawl: "They're on your trail! You'd better come to some arrangement with them." (That'll be easy…) The rest of the staff were startled, unaware of the situation.

He was becoming dehydrated by the overly powerful heating system, which he found suffocating. He decided to go out and stretch his legs, just as he was in shirtsleeves, along the wide corridors and landings of shiny white marble as far as the offices. Upon returning, some moments later, he opened the door and came face to face with McGee, who had turned round like a bull getting ready to charge. Oh! God! He hadn't even thought about the possibility. He retreated, slammed the door and ran off. Where? Not to the elevators; they were slow, hydraulic, you had to wait for them, and pull the cord… He didn't descend the deserted stairs; he flew down them (he had a choice of two), sliding down the sumptuous carved bronze banister. What luxury! He was going so fast that he didn't even stop in the foyer. He went out and ran across the road, blind to the traffic and the surprise of the passers-by. The sun was shining brightly, the snow was sparkling, and it was bitterly cold: eight to ten degrees below. And there he was in his shirtsleeves! He stopped on the corner. There was a candy-store–tobacco, ice-cream, soda drinks, coffee, odd and ends–with an open counter at right angles to the two streets, from where, under the astonished gaze of the shopkeeper, crouching and his teeth chattering with cold, with only his eyes and forehead showing above the parapet, he could watch the entrance to the building. There was McGee, scarlet faced, hair ruffled, in his pine-colored overcoat with its buckled belt, puffing with fury and looking everywhere for him! Until he gave up and walked away. The consequences of this were going to be… It didn't bear thinking about. He walked back, jaws chattering and his ears burning. If I end up with pneumonia!… He went upstairs on foot. As he entered the office, he heard the boss's voice: "Ah! It's you. McGee came back to tell you to expect him at home tomorrow morning, at eight o'clock sharp."

He woke up early, tidied the house, and so as to disguise himself, he parted his hair on the other side, put on some old glasses with metal frames–how naïve he was!–but he didn't dare dye his moustache. Maybe he could get away with it like that… It wasn't yet eight o'clock, and the door sounded as if it was being kicked in. He ran to open it. "Why did you take so long to answer?" The man was on the warpath, a bad sign. It was a modest room. In his fury, McGee blew away the shreds of rubber and cigarette ash left over from the previous night's work on the rickety table, and he prepared himself for a grilling. The same thing as always: what was his occupation, did he have any money, when did he intend leaving…

He explained himself as best as he could and with care, amid his confusion: he was a scholar, he wanted to get to know the United States, to do research, maybe even write a book–traditions-customs-institutions… And to ram it home, modestly and naively: "Maybe I'm not an immigrant like the others…"

"Oh! No? Maybe you're worse! We don't want people of your sort here!"

So that was it. It offended him, but all he could do was keep quiet. Be careful! What a devil of a man, red-faced, impulsive, informal–an Irishman, and saying such things! He might be expelled from the country, but others–adventurers, traffickers, criminals, racketeers–they would manage to stay and carry on with their business more or less unsupervised… And how strange it was that no mention whatsoever was made of the previous day's incident, the encounter and his flight, the fact that he had been caught in the act, Mr. Martinson's brazen, generous lie with him right there under the nose of authority. Why? Was it that he didn't want to complicate the investigation, compromise Martinson, who had links with big business? Well, it was better to let sleeping dogs lie! What strange people, what a strange country! Oh! America, America, when will I ever understand your secrets?!–In a word: I'm done for!

Some days later he got a phone call from his lawyer: "Didn't you tell me you were going to Canada on a business matter? Get going right now if you can, tomorrow at the latest. I've got an official letter here that I can't read you now and which tells me that one of my clients must be on the first sailing back to his own country. Do you understand? Do you UNDERSTAND?" He shouted down the phone. "I understand perfectly well! Yes, I think I'm beginning to understand … America the incomprehensible!"

He left the following morning for Canada, in her brother's car, an old Ford rattletrap. In their haste, or because they didn't notice it, they didn't even stop at the border. They caught sight of a solemn looking edifice with the air of a campus university, with cars parked round it and the stars and stripes at the front entrance. No one stopped them. "Just keep going!" he told his future brother-in-law, an inexperienced lad of eighteen. At the Canadian border post, they had to stop. He spoke to them in French. The guards remarked: "No one coming from the United States speaks it so well!" One of them only spoke *patois*. They let them through without any problem. He was carrying a letter in which a Brazilian diplomat friend offered him a job as a private secretary, in the pay of the Brazilian Treasury: without any burden, therefore, on the poor American economy! The consul in Toronto received him cordially: "This letter solves your problem!" He pushed the thick packet of documents across the desk to him: "You can take these with you, they're of no use to you." And he gave him an immigrant visa.

In their enthusiasm they went to Montreal, where the girls smiled at him as if they were in France. They took a trip through the area of the lakes, gazed in wonder at the waterfalls, and at midnight, re-entered the United States across the Niagara Falls international bridge. But entering wasn't as easy as leaving. The consul belonged to the Department of State and had no jurisdiction over them, officials from the Department of Labor; he was a lawyer, a professional, and he was coming to compete with his American colleagues. How could that be if he was a foreigner, and had no diploma from the country?! "Wait a moment," one of them told him, and he went up a coiling iron staircase that led goodness knows where, into the darkness. He dialed the phone, while he, leaning on the counter, felt in mortal danger. How much money did he have in his pocket? How could he stay and what could he do in Canada? He listened to that murmured conversation, which consisted of questions and pauses. If he was speaking to Ellis Island, their answer would surely be: "But that guy's already been given his expulsion papers!" He was in a cold sweat. The other official was admiring the stamps in his passport: "Can I take them?" "Take them all, but let me keep the visa and the consul's seal!"

The first official came down the stairs and smiled: "You can go."

They left at the double–that had been fifteen minutes worthy of Rabelais! It was a dark night, and they lost their way, singing all the while. The following morning they were in Delaware. They only got to New York at about two in the afternoon, dizzy and exhausted.

For three months, the Immigration Service, chased him with a succession of puzzled letters: when, how, where and with whom had he left the country and when, how, where and with whom had he come back in? He replied to each letter laconically and politely. No one was going to take his visa away from him! Until eventually they forgot him and left him in peace–but always far from prosperity. He didn't see the charming McGee again, and he was sad. How angry he must be. And for a long time afterwards, he continued to disseminate the hallowed propaganda of the Inter-American Press Service, in the service of D. D. Martinson, may God rest his soul.

Weekend '37

I return from my weekend, my eyes brimming with sunshine, with dense greenery, with paths through forests and grassland, with shimmering water, with pictures of bodies, their skin burnished and gleaming, their movements and bearing free and harmonious, and in my ears, I can still hear the echo of laughter and shouting from moist red mouths, the murmur of waterfalls, and of gushing streams.

This landscape, devoid of towns, houses, farms or cultivated fields, without apparent limits or any visible sign of the fruits of human toil, may lack the element of surprise, the picturesque, the intense taste and smells, the blinding sunlight, the dazzling blues, the violent and suggestive contrasts, the gentle qualities, the bucolic warmth of our country; but nowhere have I felt so deeply and intensely Nature's breath; nor have I listened with such attention to primeval silence, or breathed so much air of personal freedom.

As one crosses these empty green fields, one asks oneself where the cities are, with their smoke and fumes, their shadows and their light. There are rocky outcrops and forest mists, birdsong (certainly sharper than that with which we are familiar), and slanting shafts of hazy sunlight penetrating the quiet mystery of the glades, where, at every turn I am startled as I fancy I see emerge the last Mohican, his bare chest, tawny and muscular.

In the distance, blue mountains, more forests, green plains, the curve of a river like the thrust of a saber, and further on a lake. Over all this, clouds roll, rush onwards, spectacular, electrifying, ominous, dissolving suddenly in an epic thunderclap, or scattering in a deluge of rain. And everywhere, in the earth and the sky, there is a vastness, a feeling of endless expansion that fills a man's breast with a continental ambition, and that nowadays is illusory. There is a smell of dampness, of ripe hay, and on the ground, invisible beneath the vegetation that forms the undergrowth, scuttle animals–a stinking skunk, covered in silky fur, a brown squirrel, a golden chipmunk, speckled like a cowry, or a tortoise with a head like a vulture.

The silence is suddenly broken. As the road dips in hairpin bends, I glimpse the blue basin of a small lake framed by trees. The road, its tarred surface polished by the pressure of tires, hugs its shore. Between two dense clumps of forest, there is the shape of a narrow stretch of grayish beach, where tanned bodies lie exposed to the benefits of the sun. From the water, the cries of children and adults soar upwards as they swim, play, and frolic in carefree enjoyment. A large, brightly colored ball bounces and glides across the calm surface of the water. In the distance, there is more laughter and shouting, motor canoes draw a furrow through the pliable, blue, glass-like water, agile bodies on water-skis tear the air and the sunshine in rapid, curvaceous movements, throwing up spray from the quivering waters. Unaware of all this activity, half-dressed men, wearing panama hats or green peaked caps, pipe gripped between their teeth, dark glasses, calmly flick their fly-fishing rods in a stream that flows out into the lake nearby. On what looks like an abandoned raft, rocking gently like a cradle, a young couple lie sleeping as they drift along, their faces covered by a Mexican straw hat, intoxicated by torpor, satiated, like two people in a Monet painting. And a pristine, splendid, refreshing peacefulness flows down into the lake from the verdant heights.

Scattered across the slopes, joined and separated by the woodland, there are modest summer bungalows and some permanent residences, all made of timber. It is a colony of artists, intellectuals, teachers and white-collar workers. We are seventy or eighty kilometers from the city. The railroad is quite a long way away. Here and there, cars are parked, almost all of them older models. The village is a small one. (But I can't see any sign of the usual pointed church tower.) Everywhere, there are half-dressed children. Women walk around in simple dress (or undress), most of them in slacks or shorts and tee-shirts, the men stripped to the waist or wearing a polo-shirt, shorts or light khaki or twilled trousers that are usually crumpled. People are out shopping in the village, for it is nearly dinnertime. In front of the bungalows, people play games in the open air: football, ping-pong, garden tennis, and a type of quoits. There are wicker or canvas chairs on the grass, and people sit round in a circle, talking calmly, or take a nap, a book open in their lap.

As evening falls, after dinner, the rubbish and leftovers are burned in wire baskets, or in the ovens made of dry or cemented stone, caked with soot. (When autumn comes they will do the same with the fallen leaves.) Smoke rises slowly in the evening light and hangs like a shredded veil among the branches, growing thicker along the slopes of the hill like a forgotten mist meditating in the stillness of the air. And my thoughts turn once more to the green-blue dusk in our mountains, with the acrid smoke of nightfall…

In all of them I encounter the same joy of living, of escaping the turmoil, the same unencumbered, natural simplicity of those who possess neither serfs nor servants, the same relaxed air, the same active and meditative refuge in the bosom of a Nature that is almost totally unspoilt, or that has perhaps been reconstructed upon the ashes of the first waves of expansion. Which does not mean that there are no problems, struggles, worries or threats! This history teacher (who, when he performs pastoral duties as well as his teaching, works as many as sixty hours a week!) cuts wood with the axe of a *settler*, dreaming perhaps of an age of individualism that has gone forever; further on, a theater critic comes back from the wood, his arms full of dry twigs to burn in his hearth, for the nights are cool round here, even at the height of summer; and while a skinny little fellow of unathletic appearance, glasses perched on his nose, wearing shorts, his scruffy sandals revealing frankly ugly feet, explains to me the peculiarities of the lives of the trout that inhabit the rivers and lakes (he is a biology teacher), I steal a glance at the poet, further down the hill by the water, who laboriously carries out repairs to his launch that the harsh winter has corroded; he is a Pulitzer Prize winner with three editions of his work sold out, and a modest apartment with two and a half rooms (plus kitchen and bathroom) in Greenwich Village. All of them, as well as helping their wives with domestic chores, manage to combine manual work to a greater or lesser extent with a life of the mind. They didn't need to learn this at school, it was life that taught them. And they enjoy what they do.

The womenfolk sit around talking: about art, politics, books, their children, school, and social activities. And once their mystery has been deciphered, it is pleasant to watch these half-naked bodies, both the beautiful and the unattractive ones, without being aroused by some facile sensual instinct. Next to me, my friend from Zacatecas is put out; as his libido is not awakened by the sight of these bodies, exposed as they are, he fears he has lost his macho drive, he tells me he feels cheated, and this saddens him. I try to console him: can't you see that they are Indians? Like the ones in your homeland? We've returned to Nature... Maybe he feels more at home with the traditions that come from the Iberian side of his heritage; he does, that's for sure. Yes, maybe we are returning to a tribal form of life, to the time of Pericles, that is, assuming that the Greeks went around with so few clothes on! We are a far cry from the agora, the temples, the archon, the oratory and the gymnasium. And who knows? From among the forest glades floats the husky, virile voice of a radio commentator.

At the end of the day, the poet-caulker and the biologist-gardener invite me to attend their meeting. We all go by car, our skin and hair permeated with the smell of vegetation, with freshness and freedom, to the old barn, used for storing grain or hay, an abandoned ruin that a sculptor has converted, with his own bare hands, into a home and a studio, where comfort, simplicity, taste and industry are all combined. There are now few pinpricks of light in the dusk that has filled the forest and blanketed the lake. At the meeting, there are teachers, critics, workers, artists, employees, writers... I then realize that the City, and behind it the busy, seething world, is present with its problems, beliefs, doctrines and anxieties.

Consciousness emerges and functions in the midst of leisure, in the peace of the forest and the waters. We are members of a society that is historically removed from the primitive inhabitants, but reintegrated into Nature by means of and thanks to technology and reflection. Urban life has come to seek shelter and congregate momentarily in the middle of the woods, like some *jamboree* of the vanished autochthonous population. Men and women, sitting, crouching, standing, smoking, ask to be allowed to make their point; they speak softly, almost without any gestures, with the simple, good-humored and admirable power of expression that characterizes them, with an eloquence concentrated totally in the chosen word, in the tone of voice and in the facial expression, and for that very reason, all the more effective and meaningful. They discuss problems, and then they gather contributions for community repairs and services. The host serves cold drinks and whiskey or gin, and the aroma of coffee mingles with that of tobacco smoke. The radio broadcasts the news, and everyone listens attentively; then, there is dance music.

The holiday begins again, and there is laughter once more. The sound of other joyful voices wafts up from the darkened lake, and the wood is filled with the noise of merrymaking, and the bright lights of Venetian balloons. My friend from Zacatecas is silent and lost in thought. Maybe he would like to embark on some flirtatious course of action that would bring more concrete and immediate results!

Less than a hundred years ago, this place was still frequented by "peaceful" Indians, selling their tribal furs and artifacts to the *settlers*.

Hours later, on the train that takes me, tired and happy, back to the City, I see round about me tanned faces and the eager eyes of those still affected by their purifying immersion in Nature. Only the passengers who have come from further afield are wearing townish clothes, with hats and ties. Composure has disappeared and without it, manners are touching in their natural spontaneity. The carriages of these trains are called *coaches* (that is, they have no classes or compartments), and they are wide and long, with high ceilings, silent and air-conditioned (exaggeratedly so, just as in the summer, they are overheated to the point of suffocation). As they begin to move, they glide almost without one noticing, and stop in the same way: on bearings. There are no smells of coal or burning oil. As there is only one class, just as on most trains, with the exception of luxury or long distance services, contact among passengers is limited by their natural reserve, which is considerable. No one has brought their own snack or meal with them, so they have no food to share among their traveling companions; hawkers are continually going up and down the train advertising their sparse choice of unattractive provisions: chocolates, sandwiches, assorted nuts, ice-cream, bottled drinks. And the inevitable magazines. Some of the long-distance travelers lie asleep, stretched across three or four seats, without a thought (even while asleep) for those who get on after them and rush up and down two hundred meters of train, at their wits end, loaded down with suitcases, bags and hold-alls, trying to find a place; many of them are resigned to standing, so as not to disturb the selfish sleepers. How timid they are! They wouldn't get away with it in my country! I think to myself angrily. But soon an inspector comes and wakes some of them up to force them to give the recent arrivals a place.

For those who don't suffer from incurable hostility, traveling like this is pleasurable, like in the old third class back home, but in a carriage bathed in light, amidst the noise of conversation, laughter, and even the canoodling of young couples or lovers who kiss, or fall asleep entwined in affection and fatigue, students, employees, typists, workers, most of them immigrants perhaps, simple folk, what one might call "the people" here, if such a thing still existed. Only one distinction is made: smokers and non-smokers. As I absentmindedly look enviously at these folk, I light a cigarette. As the conductor passes by, collecting the tickets slotted into the backs of the seats of those passengers due to leave at the next station (but how can he remember with so much coming and going?), ruddy-faced and stern, an Irishman for sure, he bends over and murmurs in my ear: "If you wish to smoke, it's the third carriage from the end!" And he smiles and gives me a friendly pat on the shoulder.

In front of me, at the end of the carriage, clearly visible from where I am sitting, there is a sign: *Smoking not allowed.* Smoking is forbidden (or rather: it is not accepted…) I extinguish my cigarette and throw it away. The man could have fined me a hundred dollars (with or without jail). It's just that, unlike other countries where the law is broken all the time and no one dares to enforce it, or it can only be enforced by recourse to violence, here it is not assumed that the ordinary citizen consciously and intentionally breaks the law. Unless he is a member of the Mafia…

The Chastity Belt

Giovanni P.…., a Sicilian, appears before a court in Brooklyn to answer charges of grievous bodily harm, which he inflicted upon his wife. Asked about his motives, he explains–in an Anglo-Sicilian dialect–that his wife had violated the chastity belt that he obliged her to wear, by cutting it with a pair of scissors. The judge, the jury and the public are thrown into confusion: *A chastity belt?* What might that be?–No one knows the answer, and the Sicilian, sullen-faced, cannot, or doesn't dare to explain. The court is adjourned, and the magistracy rushes, *en masse*, to a local museum to study an example held in its collection of the (for them and by them) hitherto unseen wondrous contraption.

With their curiosity satisfied and the understandable ignorance of the upholders of Justice remedied, the case resumes:

"Why did you force your lady wife to wear such a barbaric thing?"

"Because she's from Naples and very hot-blooded!" the accused explained.

"Maybe that's because she was born near Vesuvius, no?" commented the magistrate, winking at the gentlemen of the jury, over his stern looking spectacles. Rumbles of laughter… "But is she unfaithful to you? Or do you have some reason to be suspicious?"

"None! I'm sure she's faithful to me, and she's a good girl. But prevention is better than cure, isn't it, Your Honor? That's why I punished her. In the home, it's the man who gives the orders."

When it is her turn to be heard, the wife declares that she knew where her husband hid the key to the guardian of her shame, but never went to fetch it. "And why not?" The judge interrupts her. Because this would be tantamount to betraying him, lying to him. She would only take the belt off in his presence and with his authorization. "Mmm!" went the judge. She had preferred to rebel, and assume responsibility for her act. As the leather belt was very uncomfortable, she had attacked it with the scissors and ripped it open from top to bottom. My! The blow had confined her to bed for two weeks. Oh! What a volcano Vesuvius is! Oh! What things chastity leads us to do!

After this, the court sentences the accused to three months imprisonment (suspended) and the judge gives the wife a reasoned sermon on hygiene and the rights of women.

Brooklyn still has its judges. And its chastity belts!

The Man Who Shot Down the "Hindenburg"

He was working... at least doing what he called working; he was trying out designs and colors on the huge cards of the type he had used for the portable posters in the parade a few days before. They had been greeted enthusiastically. During the procession along the streets (which had lasted the whole day), he had heard words of commendation and praise. Someone standing on the edge of the sidewalk: "It was they who discovered America, not Columbus!" Or was that what he thought he had heard? His men puffed up with pride! All of them laborers, dockers and so forth.

He was alone at home, all the neighbors were out, the building was silent, the day magnificent, with a clear blue sky—to be honest, it reminded him of Lisbon, the Lisbon of the good old times. In his linen smock, drill trousers and sandals, with his cards spread around the almost unfurnished room and his pots of paint lined up on the shaky table, he felt free, young, relaxed, and more in control of his life than in all his thirty-five years. It was time he was stealing from his working hours, but it couldn't be helped. It was a hobby. Always stealthily, like some secret vice! When he wrote, he felt like a painter, and when he painted... To hell with it! He was a hybrid. Or neither one thing nor the other. Maybe if he stuck at it?... It was the first attempt. Ever since he was a child. Caricatures, illustrations, even oils! Oh! But I'm not Picasso, nor Chagall, nor Miró, nor Matisse, nor nor nor...! He knew he was conventional, old fashioned, a realist, tendentious, representational… (as he was when writing). And so what? Each to his own, he does what he can, he amuses himself. (We all in some way or another have to stifle our anguish!) He came out of himself, expressed ideas, convictions, the feelings that assailed him. He had a purpose, or at least he thought he had. He did things which he felt were sincere, reflected his mood, were powerful and often surprised with their satirical power. The men understood it, and liked it. It was them he was addressing. (Yes, but the savages had left the posters in the street after the parade! What was it they understood? Poor souls, crushed by exhaustion. Maybe someone had caught them. The Committee members, on the platform in Union Square, had said things through loudspeakers, pointing at the posters…) Even Girona, the talented Cuban surrealist painter, liked his dawdling: *What you lack is technique!* That's why he was sticking at it. Technique. And circumstances inspired him.

As he painted, he gnawed away at himself self-critically and he sang; that was the funny thing, for it helped the rhythm of his hands. The afternoon flowed by quickly, and the sun was already sinking over in the direction of the Hudson River when the quiet of the neighborhood was shattered by a long roar that came through the air: as if a squadron of planes were flying over the West Side. Hell! Anything is possible in the current climate! He dropped his paints and brushes and leant out of one of the windows at the front of the house and looked up. He couldn't see anything. Maybe from the back! He rushed through the house, followed by the cat with its tail held high, and went and leaned over the glass-covered balcony that looked onto the rear courtyard. Twisting his neck, he saw a gigantic, multi-colored cigar that looked as if it were made of aluminum appear in the sky high over the rows of back yards between the gray three- or four-storied buildings. He recognized it straightaway from the photos in the papers (there was nothing else like it); it was the *Hindenburg* flying low, slowly, its engines roaring, displaying itself arrogantly to the astonished imperial city. It had just arrived, the first flight of the season. It was May, the weather was good and tourism was beginning again. It prided itself on its publicity (a crossing of just sixty-five hours, and these Americans, instead of boycotting it…)

He watched it in astonishment. It was, indeed, an impressive sight. On the great forward and rear rudders, a freshly painted black and white swastika shone on a bright red background, visible from many miles away. All of a sudden, the world's problems, as well as his own, welled up from deep inside him like the larva in the crater of a volcano. With his hands clenched and teeth grinding together, alone and powerless, he contemplated the airship–clear, vivid, Teutonic, functional–as it cut across the evening sky with a provocative roar. There were murmurs of admiration from windows and back yards.

His blood boiled. Without thinking, without wishing it or being aware, his eyes stared at the metallic shape of the Zeppelin with an uncontrollable magnetic force: Ah! If only he could bring it down right here and now! If only his eyes were machine guns!... For a few moments, they were more than that: two identical anti-aircraft guns firing invisible salvos, one after the other! Worse: a continuing, senseless, gush of hatred, unadulterated in all its malevolent intentions. He had become a machine, a soulless item of weaponry.

The airship passed overhead and out of sight, the clamor of its engines faded away into the general noise of the city, the people in their yards and at their windows turned indoors, and he went back to work. But he felt suddenly empty, disillusioned and listless. The cards looked awful and as powerless as he was himself. Dolls pitted against fire and steel! No, he was not a painter. And then, as the sun went down, there was no longer enough light. He was on the ground floor. He put them away in a corner, face to the wall–they didn't even bear looking at!–He screwed down the tops of the jars, put his brushes to soak in an empty cat food tin, cleaned and tidied the table, and swept the floor. He was scrupulous in the way he kept order–it was a matter of conscience: to cover up any evidence of sweat and toil. Otherwise, he wouldn't know how to start again. Later, with the lights already on, he washed his hands and face, shaved, changed his clothes, and went out, having decided to go to Nona's for a drink in order to get over the indisposition that the appearance of the *Hindenburg* had induced well over an hour before.

It was half-past-six. The spring dusk was gentle and translucent. As he arrived at Nona's, he saw a crowd of people gathered round the newsstand on the corner. The evening editions had just arrived and the piles of papers seemed to be fast melting away; people were buying them, snatching them, unfolding them, and reading them and exchanging views among themselves right there. Some accident or sensational crime, good for business. That's how they make their living, *advertising*! He drew near and managed to read the huge doleful headline:

"Hindenburg Goes Down in Flames Over Lakehurst!"

He felt a chill in his spine, a sudden numbness. The photo took up almost the whole of the front page. At a height of a little over a hundred meters, the tattered airship was plunging downwards, enveloped in flames.

From the gondolas, despairing passengers leapt to their deaths, in a blind attempt to save their lives.

He stood stock-still, unable to move, listening to the comments of those around him. Someone mentioned sabotage, and he trembled. With great effort, he dropped three cents in the dish, took a copy and walked off. He wanted to be alone with his suspicion. On the inside pages, photos showed the Zeppelin as he had seen it, hovering majestically above the Empire State, then crossing the river in the direction of New Jersey, exploding over the Naval Station, crashing in flames, and finally the huge charred, smoking frame, a pile of red hot, twisted scrap metal on the ground, next to the mooring mast. It looked like a huge crushed umbrella. How extraordinary these photojournalists are! An electric spark had been the probable cause of the disaster. Thirty-six people had died…[*]

He stopped, his brow bathed in sweat and his legs weak. A spark! Sabotage! He could see it clearly, or thought he could. Minutes before the accident, he had sprayed the airship with bullets of hatred. He had never felt anything like it, such violence in his restrained aggression. Maybe his eyes had hidden powers, it wouldn't be the first time. That's what had caused the explosion. The look he had given it. A magnetic-explosive look. He was a murderer. An arsonist! *I was the one who brought down the Hindenburg!* Terrified, he was about to run off, but he remembered his drink. He turned back, went into the bar and ordered a double whiskey, without soda, please! Everyone was talking about the incident. Leaning on the smooth dark wooden counter, he read and re-read the reports, studied the photos, and had a second whiskey. He was left in no doubt whatsoever. His hands trembled. He left.

… It's easy to imagine the rest (in his solitude he didn't speak to anybody else about it). That night he couldn't sleep. Nor on the following nights. He saw the swastika in the sky, the explosion, the innocent passengers throwing themselves out… He was burning with hatred and fear, and sweating. He got up in the darkness of night. He had lost all his well-being. He could no longer read or work. He didn't touch his paintbrushes or cards again. Nothing could distract him, he didn't even go to the cinema anymore. He would surreptitiously leave home, wearing dark glasses, so as to hide his murderous look. He wandered at random, mainly at night, through the docks, talking to himself, repeating details of the accident, haunted by unendurable images, avoiding the police… It went on for months! He even tried to fight it by having some sessions with a psychoanalyst, a German Jewish refugee. It was no good. The man seemed to be frightened of him.

Until one day...

It was right there, at the entrance of the Madonna di Pompeia church: they found him kneeling on the steps, disheveled, dirty with several weeks' growth of beard, his arms open like a cross or beating his chest in remorse, shouting incoherently and unintelligibly, rambling on about paintbrushes and the Hindenburg...

I'd better stop here. If I hadn't made it up, even I would feel sorry for him.

Note

*On the afternoon of 6 May 1937, after its first Atlantic crossing of the year, the airship Hindenburg (LZ-129) exploded and caught fire when it was preparing to be moored to the tower of the Lakehurst Naval Station, New Jersey. The United States had refused to provide the Germans with helium, and the Hindenburg was using hydrogen, which is highly inflammable. The disaster was attributed to a surge of static electricity. But the possibility of sabotage was never completely ruled out. (Author's note.)

A Chimpanzee Called Dorothy

Aman came into my office, looked around suspiciously, and sat down. He had already phoned me at the advice of the chancellery at the Consulate: "He told me you can help me, sir, and that you are in difficulties."

What a nice introduction! He started off by antagonizing me.

"Difficulties? What do they know about my life? I lead it as best as I can. But lets get to your problem."

"I have a chimpanzee called Dorothy that I've looked after since she was little and she's lived with me for a long time, in Africa. She's like a member of the family. She's extremely intelligent and understands everything I tell her. The only thing she can't do is talk. So I decided to bring her to America. She's going to be a real hit. I've already been offered eighty dollars a week to show her at a circus. But I turned it down. My Dorothy is going to earn a thousand dollars a week in Hollywood, in the films. The thing is that she only obeys my orders."

"But what does she do? Does she do tightrope walking? Is she a cyclist or an acrobat? Does she dance?"

"No, sir. I'm teaching her to write. I whisper an order to her, or show her a written word on a piece of paper, she goes to the blackboard, takes a piece of chalk and writes it."

"A chimpanzee writing! That's something that's never been seen before. Not even Koehler... But a thousand dollars a week is a lot of money. It's a star's wages!"

"That's precisely why. Dorothy is a star. What I need now is someone to help me with the publicity."

"That's where I come in."

"Exactly. I've been working things out. I rent a shop by the week in Times Square, like the gypsy fortunetellers I've seen there; I do it up, curtains and things like that, and set myself up there with Dorothy, and you, sir, as you're a good speaker and know English well, sit in the window with a microphone and explain things to the public. With the loudspeaker in the window, see what I mean?"

"Well I'm not sure. Your idea…"

"It's really good publicity for her. Just think: in the middle of the day, or at night, with all those crowds! At a dollar, or even fifty cents a time, it'll be a gold mine. Publicity is what it's all about in America. When they see it in Hollywood, I'll have them eating out of my hand."

"I'm sorry, but I somehow doubt that. It could even cheapen your chimpanzee. Film stars, to the best of my knowledge, never started out in market places or fairgrounds…"

"And what about Marilyn Munroe? Didn't she pose stark naked for a calendar?"

"Okay, yes, in the beginning…"

"Well this is only to begin with! She's costing me a lot of money. I'm keeping her at the home of one of our countrymen, in Perth Amboy, in a cage in the backyard. Fifty dollars a week! And we're two mouths to feed! Hotel expenses, transport… As I'm out most of the time, she, poor thing is all alone there and gets irritated. She's used to my company over there in the backlands! The man's scared of her. I've got to get her out of there. The shop will solve all my problems."

"So of us two, who's the one in difficulties…"

"Here you go, thinking it's a joke! You're Portuguese and that's enough. Always suspicious. If you're not interested, just say."

"I'm not joking, nor am I suspicious. I'm sorry, I didn't mean to offend you."

"So do you accept or don't you? Shall we rent the shop?"

"Yes, well… As you can see, at the moment… I have my clients, I can't leave them all of a sudden. And then, you don't want me to be an impresario, you only want me as a speaker. You'll go off to Hollywood with Dorothy, and I'll be left here watching the ships. In Times Square. Give me two days to decide."

(You can just picture me, in a shop window in Times Square, microphone in hand, bellowing from 9 till 12 and from 2pm till 6, and late into the night–*Esteemed members of the public! Ladies and Gentlemen! Children and adults! Come on in! Dorothy, the most famous chimpanzee in the world! She can read and write, works out sums in her head and will tell you your horoscope! The only thing she can't do is talk... Fifty cents a time! Free for children! Come on in one and all...Etc.!*)

The fellow left fed up with me, and thinking to himself: these useless intellectuals who don't understand anything about practical life!–So he doesn't have enough to keep the creature, turns down eighty dollars a week (if it's not a lie), in the hope of earning a thousand... how come? Yes, I've never seen her write. And how's he going to pay for the shop in Times Square (or does he hope I'll pay?)

America, Oh! America, why do you attract the world's dreamers and madmen?

Some days later I opened the evening paper and what did I see? In bold type right across the front page:

Dorothy the Chimpanzee Takes Perth Amboy by Storm!

I devoured the report, photos and all. It was she. Dorothy was setting people talking! According to the story, exasperated by her owner's continual absences, the poor animal had broken out of the cage in the Portuguese man's yard, and run away. For some hours, from street to street, rooftop to rooftop, cornice to cornice, she attracted crowds, excited the children, obstructed the traffic and disrupted that industrious and morose town on the Hudson River.

Dozens of policemen and local firemen, armed with ladders, nets, ropes and boathooks, tried in vain to grab her. Until a policeman, following the advice of a school kid, some unknown genius, no doubt a Jew, offered her a banana; Dorothy, who was ravenous, couldn't resist the bait and allowed herself to be caught without offering any resistance.

I was utterly disappointed and almost felt remorse. What would the owner say? He hadn't shown his face again or tried to telephone. But it occurred to me that this could have been one of those publicity stunts... Yes, it must have been that! A resourceful man. And I almost regretted not having listened to him.

It wasn't long, however, before I read the following, this time on page five of the *World-Telegram*:

Dorothy Faces up to the Police

After some days of enforced holiday in a police station in Perth Amboy, Dorothy was transferred to a pet-shop on Fifth Avenue, in New York. Was this promotion or relegation? It was a smart avenue... But a *pet-shop*! What could this mean? Feeling herself a prisoner, abandoned and betrayed by her owner and companion–who, in a tight fix, had sold her for a hundred dollars!–Dorothy had lost her head like any human being, and on that day, after breaking out of her cage, freed all the dogs, opened all the birdcages and trashed the entire establishment, leaving behind her a cloud of feathers, the bodies of one or two canaries, parakeets, larks and other pet birds, some of them rare, and escaped through a window, creating mayhem on Fifth Avenue at lunch hour; thousands of people of both sexes emerged from their offices to gape, there was shouting, laughter, running around, police and firemen… Fifth Avenue was blocked off as if to allow the cortege of some celebrity to pass through. Dorothy was rushing headlong towards a place in the history books! I felt a deep patriotic pride.

But New York isn't Perth Amboy, nor is Fifth Avenue Main Street. After an hour of aerial acrobatics worthy of the best primate calligraphy and of public anarchy, as she remained unapproachable, exasperated, baring her teeth and chattering furiously, and even resisting the temptation of a large piece of 'Chiquita' banana, a policeman who was no supporter of the notion of Animals-are-our-Friends, put a bullet through her heart.

And so, from the parapet of an upper floor, Dorothy fell for the last time, onto the paving stones of Fifth Avenue, the chimpanzee that had come to America to make her owner's fortune in Hollywood. The Portuguese monkey!

Bertico

"You're too white!" he shouted at me. "You have a bath and shave yourself everyday! On the day of the revolution, I'm going to kill you!" I laughed, while a cold shiver ran through my insides. One never knows with these Cubans... Always decently dressed, well mannered, and a good friend to me! When he was sober, he was an angel; he would listen to me attentively, he was appreciative of my articles (at his request, I contributed to Spanish language newspapers and magazines), he told me I had "a Portuguese irony", like Eça de Queirós, whom he had read in bad translations and admired. But after a few glasses of rum, his narrow, mild brown eyes would take on a vitreous, bloodshot glow, as they darted this way and that. He would foam at the corners of his mouth and stutter. His English, which was fluent but suffered from his incurable Cuban accent, became incomprehensible, and this made him even angrier. During the war, a policeman had come up to him on a subway station and asked to see his military registration card, which he had left at home. Confused, he lost his tongue and couldn't explain himself, and so he was arrested. I witnessed him being kicked out of a cellar bar in the Village one night for getting involved in some fisticuffs over politics. As he was being led out into the street, he threw himself head first down about twelve steps, and crashed unconscious onto the mosaic floor; but he wasn't injured.

Bertico (short for Humbertico, of course) had exiled himself in the

United States to escape the thugs of the dictator Machado, and claimed that he was a "progressive". He had witnessed death on more than one occasion, at a time when gunmen from various factions were running loose and killing for no reason at all. One never knew exactly who was the target for the shots fired. One day he was chatting casually to an activist friend of his in a railroad station, when he heard the frightful sound of gunfire, and bullets whistled past his ears; his friend was killed outright, and he only got away by the skin of his teeth. He was a journalist by profession, and he was a competent one, managing to earn a decent living in New York by writing sporting columns and radio programs beamed at Cuba, and writing captions for strip cartoons, the so-called comics that Latin America consumed in gargantuan proportions.

He had got married in Havana, I imagine out of timidity, to a woman from a Russian Jewish family he had got to know there–memories of love and politics!–and who had helped him to emigrate. She had been beautiful and was somewhat older than he was. She bore him two sweet children, who were more like her in character than him. The good lady learned to cook "Creole" food, as they call it here, large quantities of rice and beans, with tomato sauce and lots of Tabasco. He would invite lots of Latin American friends home for dinner, especially writers, artists or professionals. It was thanks to him (and to Ben, a Chilean architect and designer), that I was introduced to Orozco, who had just covered the walls of the New School for Social Research, with subversive murals, Rufino Tamayo, at that time a promising beginner, Castaño, Varreño– "he who drinks a lot," in the words of "Little Granny"–who ended up marrying a Portuguese woman, the abstract painter Julio Girona, who drew admirable caricatures for me, and the writers José Mancisidor, a pure Mexican Indian, and his compatriot, Rembao, director of the liberal protest review, *Nueva Democracia*.

His wife would cook and serve the food. The moment she turned her back, Bertico would get out the bottle hidden under the table, and the rum would be gulped down in abundant quantities. She would come back and find him drunk: "But how did this happen if they were only drinking coca-cola with their dinner!" I didn't dare to explain. He would say to her resentfully: "I hate you! On the day of the revolution, I'm going to kill you!" The poor woman turned her face away, trying to smile... As far as I know, Bertico never killed anyone. It was all due to the rum.

We had met in the good old days at a party, held in a chaotic, well-known Harlem apartment. Drunk, Bertico was sitting on the floor in the middle of the din and trying to uncork a bottle with his teeth; but he was pulling on the glass neck of the bottle and risked smashing and swallowing it. I grabbed his hand and can readily claim to have saved his life. As he left, round about two o'clock, he pulled an overcoat, which he said he thought was his, out of the incredible pile of outer garments. Shortly afterwards, when almost all the guests had left, as I couldn't find my own, I put on the only coat that no one had claimed, and it was of exactly the same material, cut and make as mine (with a fur collar), but much too big for my skinny frame.

A few minutes later, as I hurried through the dark streets in search of the subway, I ran into Bertico and his wife on a corner, he as always with his crumpled hat, and comically squeezed into my own coat! "I was beginning to feel that this one was a bit tight round the shoulders and short in the sleeves!" He said, without realizing what had happened. We exchanged coats and laughed copiously. The incident or coincidence brought us closer together.

The only person he seemed to respect, above all by keeping quiet, was *Abuelita* (Little Granny), a short lady with swollen legs resulting from some tropical illness, hair swept back to give her some height, a cheerful manner, educated and well spoken: a typical product of the Spanish-American middle class, which, while claiming to hate everything from mother Spain, has nevertheless inherited its character and seeks to preserve it from the inevitable process of "Africanization", and by swaying between two worlds and fusing them in this way, has created a culture of such originality and variety. There was something of the retired ballerina about her (although she'd never been one), and she had a good, salacious humor that defied her age, and that neither the harshness of life, nor her spinster's chastity had managed to stifle. She had come from Cuba to be near her nephew, Bertico, whom she had reared from the cradle after the death of his mother, her sister, and the "grandchildren", whom she adored and who repaid her in kind, with love. She lived a modest existence in a rented room, for in the family's apartment, there was no room for this surrogate "mother-in-law".

She told me in her gentle singsong "Creole" Castilian that Bertico's father had been a respected black senator in the mythical age of Independence and Cuban democracy. So it was from him that Bertico had inherited his Negroid features–his dark brown complexion, his tight curly hair, and eyes streaked with red–harmoniously combined with the Iberian contribution from his mother's side: the oval face, the long, aquiline nose, the high forehead, and the well formed chin; and from both sides, the character, in which gentleness and *joie de vivre* alternated with violent and rebellious impulses. He was obsessed with Cuban politics, the problem of the sugar monoculture, and Yankee imperialism.

The years went by, and our meetings became less frequent, while in Cuba, the ephemeral parliamentary democracy had given way to Batista. Bertico remained unshakeable in his convictions. His wife fell gravely ill and was interned in a hospital for incurables, where she would die seven months later. I visited her a few times in the company of her husband, whose hair was beginning to go gray, and who had learned to drive a car, overcoming his natural timidity and inhibitions to go to the Bronx every day to take the children to school or for an outing. One day, when she was already very low in spirits, she told him in my presence: "Go away. You get on my nerves!" And he, without saying a word and with dignity, left with me: "Can you see what state she's in?" The poor woman was so ill, she could no longer put up with her husband's ways.

Meanwhile, a subtle change was taking place in my friend. In reply to a colleague one day, who was quoting the *Daily Worker*, the mouthpiece of the American Communist Party, as being a reliable source, Bertico retorted bluntly: "Well, if you take everything that the *Daily Worker* says seriously!" He left him aghast. But his hatred of North American imperialism had not abated. Speaking of the future relations between Cuba and the USSR, in answer to a question of mine, he almost lost control of the car and stammered furiously, in an authentic Creole dialect: "And do you think the day the Red Army occupies Cuba, we Cubans won't kick them out!?" Bertico had changed! Except that he was still knocking back the rum.

A year after his wife's death, he was married to a Dominican woman ten years younger than he was. Hungry for his lost youth, he started going backwards. A baby soon arrived. Later, Bertico fell ill, and the doctors took one of his kidneys out, with the warning: "Stop drinking!" Little Granny had disappeared, his two adolescent sons had gone to live on their own, and I lost sight of them in the turmoil of the great American horizon. He was now absorbed by the politics of the Dominican Republic: the Trujillos, Balanguer, Bosch, and sugar, always sugar, the political and social diabetes of the islands of the Caribbean.

Sierra Maestra came, Batista went into exile, and Fidel came to power… We had stopped seeing each other. Running into a mutual friend of ours, a Cuban journalist, I asked after Bertico: "What's he saying? He must he happy, no? Is he going back to Cuba?" The friend looked at me askance: "You must be joking! He hates Fidel as a traitor to the revolution, a lackey of the USSR! He'll never go back to Cuba!"

And he really isn't going back. He's the prisoner of a dream that is now obsolete, of his own fixed ideas, of the day-to-day struggle to earn a crust, of habits, of the bitterness and the sweetness of American life, of personal ruin, of half a kidney… And not long ago, he suffered his first heart attack.

How hard it is to understand mankind.

Bridges of Dreams

In his own way, the engineer Farrusca is what we could call, without intending any offence, a specialist. He must have built a dozen and a half viaducts and footbridges, and even a bridge with stone pillars and another one with a concrete arch, both with the most elegant lines and proportions.

One day, he turned up in America, "the land of bridges", on a private study tour, independent of government responsibilities, he declared proudly, and to attend a conference in his field. But, with some hesitation, he confessed the following to me: America was a barbaric and corrupt nation, apparently idealistic but riven by materialism—a country of gangsters, judging by the films it exported, and according to the papers, a living example of the inherent defects of democracy: good, in a word, for adventurers and poor immigrants who had no culture, and were on the hunt for dollars and their daily bread.

Knowledgeable in his work, he arrived there with his eyes wide open and very suspicious, so that he wouldn't miss a thing. In New York, he was taken to see the George Washington Bridge over the Hudson River, which had only recently been opened; a creature worthy of our respect, with its six-lane highway, over a thousand meters between the suspension towers, and pathways on either side for pedestrians (who still exist today in this country of motorists). A Portuguese poet who was there at the time, poor fellow, even told him: "This bridge, sir, is like a harp with a thousand strings suspended over the river, vibrating and humming in the wind!" Old Farrusca, who is one of those people who have always thought fine words were nothing but empty prattle, looked at him out of the corner of his eye, and muttered the word imbecile between his teeth. He walked all over it, climbed the towers, crouched down and examined the rise of its arch, scribbled down calculations, and came to the conclusion that the bridge was all wrong. In California, he visited the new bridge across the bay between San Francisco and Oakland, and there all hell was let loose! I'll let him do the talking:

"Just imagine those fellows did all their calculations, the design of the bridge etc, began to build it, and when they got to the middle, what did they discover? The bridge was blocked by a rocky island and couldn't go any further! They'd forgotten about the island or hadn't noticed it! There was nothing to be done. As it wasn't possible to dynamite it, or to demolish what they had already built, they had to drill a tunnel through the rock. A tunnel, gentlemen!—and the bridge continues on the other side."

Someone tried to explain to him that there was no mistake at all; in fact, there were TWO bridges of completely different styles and designs, which met at Yerba Buena Island, where there was a naval armaments store.

"But I wasn't convinced," Farrusca replied. "Who did they think I was? Some idiot who was prepared to swallow the bridge with an island stuck in its middle?"

To close the congress, there was a huge banquet at the Waldorf-Astoria Hotel, and he was invited to speak.

"I didn't need to be asked twice! In my schoolboy English, you understand, but they understood everything, and with my pencil and notebook in my hand, I gave them some home truths: that the rise of the arch on the George Washington Bridge was wrong, and the one between Oakland and San Francisco was a glaring example of technical ineptitude. I just wish you could have seen them; they were taken aback. One of them even agreed that the George Washington Bridge might well be wrong according to what was laid down in the compendia, but that was precisely why it was a *new* bridge; that it was built to last a thousand or two thousand years, and that every weekend, more than a million cars crossed it, and goodness knows what else. But I interrupted him right away with my blunt, Portuguese frankness: I'm not interested in how many thousands of years it's going to last! For all I care it can last until the Day of Judgment… Nor how many billions or trillions of cars are going to use it; it's wrong, and no one is going to convince me otherwise!"

"I taught them a lesson. It's so that they should realize that no one can get the better of us. We may be small, but we know how to use a pruning fork too. So there you are! You can't imagine the respect they showed me after that; nor did anyone else dare to argue with me."

A patriot like that brings tears of pride to my eyes. I'm sure the Americans would have done much better if they had entrusted old Farrusca with any of the great feats of Yankee engineering that they take such pride in (and which I realize now is completely unjustified). When one day they decide to build a bridge to the Moon, the Americans or the Russians will not fail to call or consult him: in case the bridge should come face to face with some unknown planetoid that only Farrusca's experienced and skilled eye could see out there in sub-lunar space.

The Bottle of Brandy

You were three years old when, one night, the General took us and his wife, a Galician and *madrileña* by adoption, a blond woman who was elegant and liked dancing the *schottische*, for dinner in a tavern on Ferry Street, on the Lower East Side, almost under the Brooklyn Bridge; in a maze of streets since demolished to make way for dehumanized open spaces and anonymous blocks of brick and concrete in uniformly straight lines. The area, in the immediate vicinity of the City Hall, was, in days gone by, characteristically bourgeois. In the same street was the workshop of a Galician tailor, my one-time neighbor, who proudly referred to me as a "fellow countryman". He had lived for some years in Lisbon, which he recalled with fondness, and he spoke Portuguese quite well. It was he who, with great care and taste, made the costumes for the dance companies of José Greco and Carmen Amaya, and, if I'm not mistaken, the Antonio and Rosita duo, too. One day, he made me put on the costume of a slim gypsy–tight trousers with a high waistband, a folded sash, and a jacket embroidered with silver–I could almost have been a bullfighter! Laughing, I tried a couple of dance steps in front of the mirror. "Ah! You're a born dancer!" The good Galician exclaimed, clapping his hands. I was being vain. Already in his fifties, seeing me dance a *Malagueña*, Paco Lorca, the Poet's brother, shouted to his friends at the party: "Look at Miguéis, see how he dances! His rhythm, his footwork... Miguéis is a dancer!" An Andalucian medal of honor that even today I still rejoice in. And what else can I salvage from the ruins? You even saw me dance two days after the tragedy… Life is made up of so many things! And not all wisdom is learnt from books.

People tell the story of an Irishman, who lived for a long time further up on Delancey Street, but who one day went back to Donegal. However, haunted by his memories of America, he returned some years later to Delancey Street. When he arrived, he was astonished to see that all the old signs and family nameplates had disappeared; all the names were now Jewish ones from Eastern Europe. Going up to an old man with a long gray beard and a round black hat like a rabbi's, he asked: "What's happened to the Irish? Where have they gone?" Raising his eyes, tired from reading the Tora, the old man replied: "Ah! And where have all the Indians gone?…"

We ate fried baby hake with their tail in their mouth, with salad and rough red wine, and at about midnight we went up from the basement to the bar, an old Downtown café, with dark carved woodwork, beveled mirrors and engraved glass–relics of a New York that was a ruin before it even got old, as Lévi-Strauss would say. We were fearful that the police might see us there, with a young child, and reprimand us or take us to court! But who is it that can resist the amiable commands of a general, even a vanquished one?…

The two of us leaned against the solid counter of polished mahogany, and he ordered a bottle of the best Jerez brandy for us. He filled my glass and we talked. After a while he asked the owner of the café, a sturdy Galician, to sing us some songs from his native land. The man didn't need to be asked twice; with his sleeves rolled up his hairy arms and his hands on the counter, with his baritone voice, he launched forth into melodies from the Galician hills that filled that decadent and formerly puritan quarter with nostalgia. And me too! A policeman came and looked in at the door and stood there listening and smiling. He was known to them and didn't ask any questions.

As we talked, and with the help of the songs, the brandy gradually disappeared; the General drank the lot. My glass remained half full. For years afterwards, he would repeat to me: "D'you remember, Miguéis, that night we drank a whole bottle of brandy, just the two of us?" What a memory of unequally shared responsibilities! The little Galician blonde ended up running away with a sweet-talking dark-skinned Cuban, and for some time the Department of State (Nansen), refused to renew their married couple's passport they held as exiles, until he told them where his wife was: "How should I know where she is?! Send the FBI to Cuba to investigate!" Even today, I wonder what became of her, as she was beginning to look old beyond her years.

By that time, the General had severe liver problems. Seeing him later struggle against the pain of the heart attack that killed him, I couldn't prevent myself from recalling with sadness the area and the past that had been demolished. And the brandy I hadn't drunk!

But what am I trying to say, if I am trying to say anything at all, with these fragmented images in the many sided mirror, if I sometimes feel like a man who, standing before a moving, concave wall, were endlessly depicting a panoramic and chaotic scene, ignorant of where it all began or where it is going and how it will end, if it does indeed end, but determined to grasp the reality of its presence in a world I cannot know or embrace except within the restricted boundaries of the moment I am portraying; and if the problem with literature nowadays is the concern with non- or anti-style, with a hatred of words, form, sense, coherence, and meaning?… This is a problem that I certainly hope will be resolved when literature is reduced to something with blank pages, or, as would seem already to be the tendency, with unintelligible graphic signs, tastefully distributed over the paper. By that time, we shall have achieved Absolute and Total Expression–unreality, non-sense, the absurd–and along with it, the complete happiness of our readers who will have been born sleeping and will want to continue to live their lives sleeping, that is, if they are indeed alive.

In the Boarding House

The man with the beret and wrapped in the cape was sitting against the wall, next to the little open stove upon which the *chouriço* sausages were cooking, dripping fat onto the burning coals and spreading an acrid, excruciatingly appetizing smoke. This was the only source of heat in the whole building. From the door that opened onto the hall and the stairway, there blew an icy draft. I looked at him again. In the darkness of the house, his features were barely distinguishable; thin, drawn and haggard, with a still black mustache that drooped down at the ends, and a few days' growth of beard, he seemed vaguely familiar to me. Silent and coughing, he looked at his companions from the depth of his sunken eyes. They moved around, talking loudly and laughing, arguing with one another by shouting and gesticulating. I had difficulty in understanding them. They were stevedores, seamen, diggers and shovelers, strong, crude manual laborers: my people. In a corner, grouped round an empty barrel, some of them were playing a noisy game of poker, and they swore and slapped their cards down forcefully. The idleness of Sunday, the bustle and noise, the evocative smell of roasting *chouriços,* the bottle being passed round, everything gave me a sad feeling of comfort, a mixture of nostalgia, well-being and privation. I don't know what drew me to that boarding house in West Street, next to the docks: some information I needed on their behalf, and no doubt my own curiosity. It was winter, the blizzard had lasted all night, and the deserted streets were covered with snow that the northwesterly wind was sweeping along in swirls, piling it up on the sidewalks and against the harsh, impenetrable fronts of the buildings.

Costa went over and offered him a piece of white bread with a slice of *chouriço*, which he declined by shaking his head. When Costa returned, I touched him on the arm: "What's wrong with him?–Oh! He's got pneumonia. He's been at home for three days. He was getting bored all alone up there in his room and asked them to bring him down, so that he could be with people.–Why don't you take him to the hospital? The Saint-Vincent, just round the corner... He needs treatment!–The doctor was here, yesterday. But he doesn't want to go to any hospital. Let alone one with nuns! He says he'll get over it. It's not the first time."

Something hurt deep inside me; was it the callous indifference of men–or could it be their stoicism? The sick man was looking at us suspiciously, aware that we were talking about him. He must have been about fifty. It was then that I recognized him...

... Some time before, there was a committee meeting in the Club's kitchen. It was already nearly midnight, and a pale man, with graying hair and a black, drooping mustache, came and leaned against the doorpost, looking at us and listening, without saying a word. He stayed like that for a long time, gazing at me with his solemn eyes. Why was he studying me so insistently?

In the end, although feeling unwell, so as not to offend, I accepted a glass of beer, said goodbye and left. The Club was on the ground floor of a block of dwellings on Prince Street. In the dark entrance hall, I was afflicted by stomach cramps and nausea, and I made for the restroom at the back of the building–a narrow, badly lit cubicle, painted green, with ancient plumbing and sanitary equipment, but rigorously clean. The pains were getting worse and becoming intolerable, as if a knife were being twisted in my insides. Sitting there, bent over, groaning quietly and sweating, in mortal agony–it must be appendicitis–I suddenly heard confused but familiar voices. I looked up and realized they were coming from the kitchen along the metal ventilation shafts. I bit my lip so that they wouldn't hear my groans, and listened hard–because it was after all a distraction. I recognized Costa's authoritarian voice. Then a low, muffled voice, that matched perfectly the face of the stranger who had stared at me so long and so blankly: "Do you know him? Do you know who he is? How did he end up here? Be careful, because these smart types, when they start frequenting people like us, it's either to get their hands on our dollars, or it's to spy on us! I don't like that face of his, and as for his glasses!" Costa's voice could be heard again, unusually reflective and slow: "He's not a bad man. Apparently he was a teacher back home. He helps us out, writes the programs and pamphlets, articles… And his wife's a good sort, she organized a sewing group, fixed up some holidays for the kids in the country…" (Knowing me so well, how feebly he was defending me!)

The conversation continued, but became less easy to hear–they had moved away from the ventilation pipe. In the midst of my suffering, aggravated by my suspicions, I continued in a cold sweat for a few more moments. Fearful that they might come and find me there and suspect that I had heard their conversation, the moment I felt some relief and capable of walking, I dragged myself as best as I could to the Subway on the corner of Sixth Avenue. I must have got home at about two o'clock. I took a tablet and went to bed, while the pains became less acute. On the following day, the doctor who came to see me ventured timidly, after his examination: "It may have been appendicitis…"–and he didn't do anything.

I went back to work the very same day, and to my normal routines. But I was living with my nerves encased in barbed wire.

I looked at the poor unfortunate, who suffered without complaining. His solitude pained me, and not only his, but that of all those men who had no family, and even that of myself, who had one. They got together, and I sought them out, possibly out of the belief that strength lies in numbers. But when all the zeros are added up, the result is a greater zero still… I asked Costa: "What does he do? Has he got a job?– Oh! He was on the fishing boats for a few years, and before that, during Prohibition, he joined the people dealing in rum. In Rhode Island. He did well for himself! He's left that now and he wants to open a fish store. With his savings."

I gave him one last look (of farewell), and left. The snowstorm had ended, but the wind from Canada continued to gust furiously. A giant bulldozer with a mechanical scoop was clearing the roads, where one or two trucks and many cars had become imprisoned by the snow, in grotesque positions in front of the warehouses and sheds. The dirty brick façades looked unexpectedly pure under a layer of snow and the glittering icicles that hung from their eaves. The temperature must have been about fifteen to twenty degrees below zero. I went home through ghostly quiet streets and intersections. Alone. The man with the cape and his suspicious look was also alone, back there among comrades who were no longer so: with his savings hidden perhaps in his mattress, and his bank book under his pillow. Without any visible heirs: only maybe his mother, back in Murtosa or in São Paio da Torreira, waiting for him–or for his death certificate. Such were the fates! But I had mine too, and I continued to defy them. And I thought, smiling to myself, as I jumped over heaps of snow: *"Poor us, who have to go on living…"*

Bon Voyage, Carlos!

That morning, I was making preparations for the fourth or fifth time for my final return, when I was interrupted by a phone call. I immediately recognized the high-pitched, almost childlike voice, tremulous as if weeping: "I've got bad news for you... Father..." Her words were cut by a sob. "No, no!" I said. "Surely not! It's not possible! Only a few days ago..." (I was lying: I hadn't seen him for some weeks, even months and I felt bad.) "But it's true!" The waiter from the night-club found two or three days' worth of trays piled up outside his bedroom door, untouched... He rushed to call the boss and the police. They found him lying peacefully in bed, his eyes closed, his hands crossed over his chest. He was cold and stiff. He'd been like that for two days... I understood why she was crying and tried to comfort her. "Are you sure it wasn't suicide?–Absolutely! Did they carry out an autopsy? The coroner came, examined him, and wrote out a certificate: emphysema.–Can I go and see him? Or go to the funeral?–No! He left instructions: no religious service and no accompaniment. Cremated, and his ashes thrown to the wind from the top of the bridge over the Narrows... It's all been taken care of!" (Lord! Faithful to the sea even in death!). Even I felt shocked. It wasn't as if I hadn't suspected something for some time: the breathlessness, the acute sensitivity, a weakened heart, and he obstinately avoiding going to see my doctor, a specialist! "Always so alone! You were such a good friend to him! He talked so much about you! Please keep in touch whenever you can!" She concluded and hung up. Everything was over! It was the end. Will I ever see her again? What a close watch he kept on that daughter of his! He left her the discotheque, the junk; in particular some glassware that passed for "antiques", for the shop he intended opening. Poor Carlos!

We hadn't known each other long. A mutual friend had introduced us, a Portuguese who had just opened a shop in the Village selling Portuguese "curios". Carlos must have been three or four years older than me, and I was in my early sixties at the time. I was somewhat circumspect in my first impressions. I was even suspicious of the special treatment he accorded me. Having read some of my stories that I had given him (something unheard of among the Luso-Americans I encountered there), he told me one day over the phone: "To me, you are a God!" Only later did I realize he had the embittered severity of all those who are disillusioned or frustrated, and had merely discovered in me yet another reason for his "Portuguese-is-best" attitude. He was one of those frighteningly fanatical Portuguese patriots of the sort one only finds abroad, unfamiliar with our true needs, and proud of faded glories...

But contact with him soon erased my initial, unjustified impressions. We became friends (conversational ones above all), despite–or maybe precisely because of–our great differences. At that time he was a manager (after having been partner and proprietor) and master of ceremonies at a restaurant-nightclub specializing in Spanish dancing and warbling, beloved of certain members of the middle class, people, like the artists themselves, more mediocre than those at the old Salão Foz of glorious memory (glorious because it was situated in the Calçada da Glória), in the palace of the same name. All the hackneyed dross of Spanishness passed through there: the Hispanic world, with its unequalled abundance of folklore, is sometimes repulsive in its vulgarity. The women in the nightclub, some of them clearly whores–Spanish, Cuban, Argentinean, Puerto Rican, Dominican–and other Hispanic females of low breeding (but no black women, for they weren't allowed in)–were attracted by his status as an impresario, or perhaps by his nocturnal pallor, his cold, clear green eyes and authoritarian ways, which lent him the air of a potential pimp. I don't know whether he desired any of them. I sometimes got the impression he found them repugnant. Or is it that men who despise women have more luck with them? Unlike so many elderly men, he rarely spoke about females: maybe for fear of putting me off? He was a man of wide build and a paramilitary stiffness, his jaws tight as if he were continually grinding his teeth (which is how he spoke with a thick Madeiran accent). His eyes were the color of still water, inexpressive but inquisitive, his face pale–due to age or illness, but which must have once had the type of golden tan that fascinates women. His expression was taciturn and severe, and for me he had the particular bearing of one trying to cover up a secret feeling of inferiority.

One night, he invited me to have dinner with him and an insignificant Argentinean woman who was a member of the "ballet" and who devoured him with her sultry eyes. At one stage, on the pretext of having some tasks to do, he left us alone together. The girl, consumed with jealousy, followed him with her ravenous gaze and didn't even look at me. We didn't exchange a word. Uncomfortable with such company, and as she wasn't my "type", nor did she hold out any other attractions, I answered her silence with a: "For heaven's sake, don't feel you have to stay here with me!" She jumped up without saying *gracias* and walked off, leaving the (detestable) dinner unfinished. What a sigh of relief! (I saw her dance later; she had no talent whatsoever.) How had such a sensitive man learnt to live among such fauna?

When he returned to the table, I asked him: "Why did you leave me with that girl? I didn't come here for women, and much less of that sort! She hated me, and rightly so." Carlos was disturbed, as if he had committed a *faux pas*. And indeed he had! Did he expect me to take her off to bed? (Where?) Or that I would keep her company?

As far as I knew, he had been married three times, and had a stunningly beautiful daughter to whom he introduced me subsequently, but he now lived alone in a modern apartment in the same building as the nightclub: a spacious bedroom-cum-living-room, a narrow kitchen and bathroom of a similar size, this latter papered with huge, brightly-colored posters featuring naked and near-naked women in provocative poses of depressing vulgarity. "And do you show this to your young daughter?!" "She doesn't find anything strange. Besides, she respects my tastes! This new generation…" The living-room, literally packed with furniture and junk, contained a huge collection of Fado, Flamenco and Cante Hondo, his great passion–and endowed with all manner of stereophonic equipment, about which I understand absolutely nothing, and therefore hate. Occasionally, ignoring my protests, he would inflict upon me the torture of having to listen to his records, which at that time could be guaranteed to make me feel sick. I find nothing more tedious and repetitive than so-called Andalusian "music"!

Carlos was the illegitimate son of a Portuguese military man, from a good Madeira family, who had fled to California after the disaster of

31 January 1891. A neighbor and friend of the illustrious Burbank, like him he became a lover of select and crossbred vegetables. He was married in Portugal, and as he couldn't get a divorce, he set up home with a young Irish woman, who died only a few years later after falling down a flight of stairs leading to their vegetable garden, leaving him a young son of less than five years of age. Not knowing what to do with him, the father placed him in the care of a spinster sister of his who lived in Funchal (and later, Lisbon), and who brought the child up as if he were her own. This explains his strong Madeira accent, his blind patriotism, and the indelible Portuguese nostalgia that marked him to the end of his life. He told me, for example, that round about the time of the Fifth of October (1910), as he was living in Belém, he decided to accompany the Second Cavalry Regiment (known as The Queen's Lancers) into Lisbon, and one of the soldiers, taking pity on him for doing the journey on foot, hoisted him up onto his horse's hindquarters, and so carried him right into the center of what by then was a victorious revolution.

Later, he lived with his aunt on the slope of the Rua Marques da Silva, near the Almirante Reis (names that he had forgotten). As a gangling youth and high-school pupil, he would slip out at night through his bedroom window and vault the railings of the front gate. He would roam around, fascinated, listening to the strumming of guitars in taverns and learning to admire Fado singers and prostitutes, with whom he would become familiar later in life. He showed me a photo of himself at that time, in which he displayed all the silly signs of adolescents when trying to pose as adults. He was sixteen years old when his father summoned him to the United States, to give him an education "worthy of a man". But sadly, the soldier died soon afterwards, leaving him a paltry inheritance that was swallowed up by the taxman and the executors of the will, leaving the lad completely destitute. He never revealed to me why he hadn't returned to Portugal to live with his aunt from Funchal, who was still alive.

Repatriated thus into orphanhood, without friends or resources in the land where he had been born but was a stranger, endowed with an insufficient education that was strictly Portuguese and alienating, and above all yearning for love and care, he suffered the usual post-adolescent religious crisis, and turned his attention to what seemed to him to be God, the Father of all... So he entered a monastery belonging to some order or other in Southern California, as a student and novice. He wanted to become a friar, to be ordained, to live for religion and make his living from it. Before long, he was assisting the prior at mass in the little church belonging to the monastery, whose membership amounted to little more than twenty. He thought he had found some shelter from life's uncertainties.

Until one Sunday, while he was reciting with the reverence of an acolyte, passages from the Epistle and the Gospel, he noticed a young girl in the first row of the congregation, looking at him intensely, following every movement he made. This disturbed him, and he felt his heart pounding. The image of her was going to fill his fantasy and wouldn't let him sleep the following night, nor a couple more after that. Although he felt guilty of sin, he began to peep at her. She, for her part, never missed Sunday morning mass, always going through the same genuflections and never taking her eyes off him. He had never thought himself worthy of such attention. He didn't try to find out her name, who she was, whether she had a family, where she lived, whether she came alone or accompanied. No sooner did he approach the altar enclosure than his eyes shot like arrows in search of her and their looks entwined with one another in mid air, festooning the little church. In vain did he beg God to free him from this cult of sin. The truth was that he was uniting within one single act of contemplation, his love of God and his nascent love of life and womankind; for him, it was a sweetly novel experience. He could now vest his adoration in a real live human being and lavish upon her his sweetest and most secret thoughts. The orphan's heart, until then empty, was now full to overflowing. He loved her passionately, with a Portuguese love, with all his sensuality transposed into purity, just as the asceticism of the Order required of him.

He would spend the week in a state of anxiety, obsessed, distracted from his studies, from his duty to fast and pray, waiting for Sunday, so as to continue that conversation devoid of words and feel the hitherto unknown and unique caress of a woman's gaze. They never exchanged a single word, not even a compliment. Not even a smile. Everything between them was a secret. The only public thing, though invisible, was that ardent, furtive look.

Some months went by in this way. One afternoon, at the height of a Californian summer, shut away in his cell, absorbed in the interpretation of a particular theological enigma, it occurred to him that he should consult his superior and spiritual director, to whom he had never dared confess his sin, something that made it doubly unpardonable. He was an Irishman of little more than thirty years of age, ginger-haired, good-looking, merry and talkative—in short a priest who was well liked by his parishioners. Barefoot as he was, the novice walked down the cool tiled corridor to the cell occupied by his superior. He found the door ajar, open just a crack, which saved him from knocking and possibly waking the priest from his customary siesta. He paused to listen for a moment and heard the sound of low murmurs; maybe he was at his prayers. He decided to interrupt them—and that was his mistake; taking his courage in his hands, he gently pushed the door…

The sight that met his eyes made him feel as if he were dying on his feet; sitting astride the jovial prior in his rustic Mexican chair of plaited straw, held tightly in his arms, her thighs bare and belly joined to his, was the young girl who had been the target of the apprentice monk's Sunday contemplations and nocturnal fantasies. They were kissing each other ardently amid the stifled giggles he had taken for prayers! The silence and the burning mid-afternoon heat in the calm of the adjacent gardens and orchard enveloped the little monastery in a peace that lent itself to religious exaltation or the voluptuousness of sin. That instant of abomination destroyed in a flash the love of God and Faith in the novice's heart, his ideals, trust in mankind and in the purity of earthbound love, and made him decide there and then that, in the full blossom of his youth, he should set his life on another course, towards another future.

No one had seen or heard him. He retreated slowly, closed the door silently, and tiptoed back to his cell, feeling more alone than ever. He shut the door behind him, and it was then that he exploded in a sudden, demented, uncontrollable rage, of the sort that only a feeling of utter hopelessness can unleash in a chaste soul devoted to pure love. He tore down the sacred images that adorned the whitewashed walls, and that he was wont to pray to, and ripped them into a thousand shreds; he swept from the shelves of the modest pine bookcase all the works of Theology, Hermeneutics and Hagiology that he had venerated, and along with them the thick Latin lexicon, tearing them apart with a strength he didn't know he had, scattering them across the tiled floor. All except for one; strange, isn't it? One he was in the habit of leafing through with love and respect: a copy of *The Lusiads*, in the cheap school edition he had originally read. He ripped up the straw bed, sheets and blanket, the mats, and even the cassock he wore. Standing among the wreckage, he put on the layman's clothes he had arrived in, and which he had kept hanging on a peg, but which now barely fitted him. As his old shoes were now out of commission, he stuffed his feet in the sandals issued him by the Order. Then he tied his few possessions in a bundle and leaving the cell in an infernal mess, which seemed to mirror his confused soul, he left the monastery, resolved never to return to that place where he had lost everything, and he set off into the vastness of what was still the semi-desert of Southern

California.

For days and nights he traveled through those barren lands, along tracks lined with agaves and aggressive looking cacti, or the modest plantations of the local folk, generally mestizos of Indian and Mexican ancestry, who never refused him a hunk of God's bread or a drop of water, scarce though it was; nor shelter under a simple thatched roof, in a shed full of hay or a corral, when he wasn't happy to bed down in the den of a coyote or some other wild animal, or even in some ditch under the open sky. No one chased him away or shouted at him. They would say, "God be with you!" And he, moved, felt more removed still from that dead company. He encountered no men in uniform, nor did it occur to him that the authorities might be looking for him. He had taken a decision. He wouldn't be a monk, nor would he take holy orders. He wouldn't remain chaste or God-fearing.

Inexplicably, however, maybe because he was repentant and subconsciously praying for it, he found himself once again at the monastery some weeks later, without knowing how he had got there. He knocked at the door in rags, famished and thirsty, his sandals in shreds, dirty and covered in dust, the beginnings of a beard on his haggard face, searching for the Father he lacked or the Mother of whom he had no memory. It was like the story of the friar who was three hundred years old, except that here, the opposite happened and he was refused the shelter he asked for: he was a tramp, an unbeliever whose name they neither knew nor remembered. The prior thus erased at one go the memory of the rebellious novice and the stain of his own sin. It didn't even occur to him to seek out his true love, who no doubt lived in the nearby village.

He was about seventeen. A Portuguese at large in the world, without family–he would never again hear from his aunt who was now living in Madeira–nourished on legends and folktales about sea voyages and conquests, carrying Camões under his arm and some Jack London in his head, he decided to become a cabin-boy in the merchant navy. He got a job on one of the many four-masted clippers that still plied the route between the Pacific Coast and Australia or New Zealand, carrying machinery and heavy goods on the outward journey and returning with cargoes of exotic wood. Discipline in the merchant navy was harsh and brutal at that time. Between God and the sea, the captain's power was absolute. Little more than an adolescent, he experienced all the horrors of working conditions in the navy, the low pay, the hard wooden bed amid the promiscuity of the hold, and–young and good-looking as he was–the predatory persecution of the crew, deprived of women during the long months at sea. The slightest misdemeanor merited a lash of the whip across the back and a ration of bread and brackish water for days on end. To console himself, he would re-read Camões and think of Fernão de Magalhães, the first man to dare confront that empty expanse of mountainous waters.

"Seamen nowadays," he would tell me, "with their soft mattresses and a berth in a cabin, eight hours on duty maximum, food fit for first-class passengers, princely salaries, holidays, unemployment subsidies, insurance against all risks and into old age, they can't imagine what life was like at sea!"

In spite of all this, the Sea became his love, his spiritual home and his religion. He was a sailor for about thirty years. When he was still a mere seaman, lashed to the wheel as an assistant to the helmsman on night watch, the great waves of the Pacific would wash over him in times of storm. In the seas off China and Formosa, he saw the legendary giant bats fall as if from the sky and land on the deck, brought down by the typhoon. And so he grew to maturity and became a man. Gradually, he was promoted to boatswain, pilot, purser and first-mate, but he never got as far as captain because of his weak eyesight. At the time we got to know each other, he told me that when he was still young, he had jumped ship in Samoa, and stayed there for a long time, living with the natives, fishing in the gentle streams with a sleek bamboo spear, eating the fruit that bountiful nature offered, and cohabiting happily with a woman that a chief had provided him with. How nostalgically he described that phase of his life, lived according to the laws of nature, his best years of all! Until he was reported to the American authorities (by that time rulers of the islands) for "corrupting the natives", by whom he had been assimilated. In spite of the protection they gave him, hiding him in the less accessible villages of the interior, he was arrested by the Marines, deported back to the United States, and released. This explained his nickname, "Duke of Samoa".

I believe it was while he was still in the navy that he married a Portuguese woman in New England; I don't know anything about this marriage, which didn't last long. By this time, he was getting on in years, and with a tidy sum of money saved, he made friends, on one of his periodic trips to the British Isles, with a family from Aberdeen, Scotland, who owned an antique shop. On one of his visits, he fell ill and had to remain ashore. The couple put him up and, for a nurse, gave him their daughter, a beautiful, bashful blonde, like a character out of one of the old gothic novels. She once more gave him a taste of "the milk of human kindness"–and of love. They fell for each other and got married, after which he took her off to the United States.

The aunt from Madeira had died some years before. Carlos built his own house on the right bank of the Hudson, far from the bustle of New York, and there they had a son and a daughter who would later rival her mother in beauty. He continued to work for the same great transatlantic shipping company but now held a post in maintenance services. This was how he came to visit Spain and Portugal–which would bring about his transformation. On successive visits, he traveled all over the country, fascinated to such an extent that he eventually returned to his teenage habits–frequenting taverns and folk connected with Fado, all those blatant expressions of sentimentality that are offered returning Portuguese, deceiving them with appearances and making them believe that a bohemian soul is the essence of their nation. It was a honeymoon. He spoke to me nostalgically of the friends he had made in those circles, especially in the Solar da Alegria, a den of Fado singers of both sexes where, among other incidents, he had witnessed the fatal shooting of a "fadista" by his rival over a prostitute, whose earnings he lived off: "By the stairs, just a few feet from the table where I was sitting!" The crime of passion was quickly hushed up. Having some money at his disposal– rich as far as the locals were concerned–he set himself up as a patron of impresarios and above all "practitioners" of the so-called national song. This was a milieu he would never want to leave. While he was there, he also met the great Hermínia and Amália[1], at the time a humble singer in the night life of the popular quarters of the city. (Years later, he would see her, by this time at the height of her fame, in New York, where–to his great pride!–she agreed to sing for a group of friends at his nightclub.)

The Company eventually appointed him to a very well-paid post in Spain, that also took in Portugal. During the civil war, he witnessed, with horror, the atrocities committed in Anadalusia: "I can tell you I saw men and even women buried alive up to their necks, and then murdered by having their heads smashed by kicks or rifle butts!" His love of their regional song and dance didn't prevent him from attributing the cruelty of Spaniards to a "cowardice" from which the Portuguese didn't suffer...

Once he had retired, and with some money at his disposal, he opened a discotheque–possibly the first in the country–in Massachusetts. But his Scottish wife detested going out at night, the bohemian lifestyle, and "folk" music, and as his children were growing up, he decided to get a divorce. It wasn't long before he got married again, this time to an Ameri- can woman who drove him mad and made his life hell. She was a tyrant and had a terrifyingly provocative libido: "It was enough for me to touch her with the tip of my finger, and I'd feel an electric current running right through my body! But I never really loved her…" (She now lived in Hawaii, and they still remained on friendly terms.) She squandered money and caused him to have a serious nervous breakdown, and in the end, in exchange for his freedom, he gave her the house, library, car and a good share of his considerable savings. He just kept the discotheque, which was his livelihood. (Let me comment, at this point, on how strange it is that we think we know people from whose life we merely gather one or two casual incidents!)

He returned to New York, and it was then, with his last bit of money, that he opened the restaurant-nightclub in the Village. But in spite of his nose for it and his air of authority, business didn't go well, and so eventually he accepted a Spanish couple as partners—the wife a Puerto Rican, the husband possibly from Spain itself. Some years later, he passed the concern entirely over to them, while he remained merely the manager and master of ceremonies. It was there that we became acquainted. One night, in his home, he introduced me to his daughter, a single girl of eighteen or nineteen, who often visited him and showed him great affection. Agnès—for her mother; for her father, she was Inês, the one from *The Lusiads*—she spoke no Portuguese or Spanish, but in spite of the marked differences between them, she loved Fado, Flamenco and Cante-hondo with the same fervor. She would spend whole evenings listening to them on the complicated stereo system. She didn't want to live with her mother who, virtuous and faithful to her former husband, hoped that he would relent or be cured, and return to the marital fold (either that or die so that she could marry again), and she couldn't live with her father because she didn't want to give either parent the privilege of her preference. So she lived alone in New York, in a small apartment on 29th Street. Carlos said to me: "Guess what number!" And I replied laughing: "319!" He looked at me aghast: "What?! How did you guess?" "That's easy: because the mere coincidence of it being the same as mine would make it exceptional or miraculous in your eyes!" He sat there for a few seconds looking very serious, and in the end said: "What a Sherlock Holmes you are!" This must have reinforced our friendship…

I didn't want him to notice my pallor, nor did I dare confess that I had seen her once some months before, and been transfixed by her. Nor could I have foreseen at the time the strange relationship that the future would establish between us. Agnès had a rare, luminous beauty, with clear blue eyes, and an abundance of silky, golden hair. She was tall and slim, with a body that was supple, judging by the movements she made as she listened to the rhythms of Andalusia. "She's the image of her mother at that age!" Carlos would say, sad but proud. "But our Portuguese friends, with their Don Juan mentality, swarm after her like bees round a honey pot! They think they're irresistible, but she doesn't pay them any attention! She'll have no shortage of offers from men!" He guarded her jealously. I told him: "Your daughter is stunningly, almost prohibitively beautiful!" He threw me an almost irritated look: "Prohibitively? What do you mean by that?" "Merely that she inspires in us the same admiration we might feel for a goddess beyond our reach!" He was satisfied with my explanation.

She was a decorator, with a highly-paid job in a company specializing in decoration, tapestries and fabrics, whose cards she designed and colored. Agnès had her future secured and her father was proud of her for this. Once or twice, she invited me to have dinner with him in her little apartment. She would sometimes give me a deep, thoughtful look of incomprehension. Her incomparable blue gaze pierced me with a cold, radiating strength capable of melting metals and rocks… I had never seen such a look in any woman; stunning, glowing, it seemed to plumb my innermost thoughts. Even today, as I write this, I can never remember being able to detect any flickering of feeling, emotion, or desire. At the most, something occasionally made it still clearer and more gentle.

(… It was in a very busy street, in the half-light of approaching night, before the street lamps came on. Trapped from afar by a projector or the klieg-light in a film studio, she stopped, her eyes wide open, unmoving, like an idol or some supernatural being, staring into the source of light that bathed her. Was she awake? Or merely fascinated? I stopped too, hypnotized by that unknown gaze. The street lamps came on and the projector was extinguished, the magical moment evaporated, and she melted into anonymity without having seen me, nor I her, although I had tried to follow her in the crowd. I was intoxicated, without realizing immediately that I was love-smitten. For some time, I assumed I had been the victim of a hallucination or some supernatural vision… Nor could she have recognized me when we were introduced. I kept my astonishment to myself.)

Round about that time, business at the nightclub went into decline, not only because the clientele dried up, but also due to the rows between husband and wife, for she, despite being a truly awful singer, insisted on performing alongside the professionals. "She's going to kill the business!" Carlos would tell me, dispiritedly. He himself was weighed down by his emphysema and in spite of the financial constraints in which he lived, had paid a small fortune to purchase the exquisite matador's suit that had belonged to the mystic and legendary Manolete, not long after his sudden death, and when we saw the film, consisting largely of stills, on his life and career. He had kept it in a glass case like some precious museum exhibit, or the mummified body of some pharaoh. "I may have to sell it, and I'd find that really hard! But who's going to want to buy something like that? My abiding passion!"

Disillusioned by the business that he had once loved, he took advantage of an even deeper rift between the couple to tender his resignation, and he looked for a less demanding job. But what could this sixty-year old former sailor do? A singer friend of his, who was still very much in demand, Vincente López, alias Vicente Lopes, a Portuguese who passed himself off as a Spaniard because "a Portuguese name isn't a business proposition in this country", got him a position as a head waiter in the cabaret of the large hotel where he performed. But the work was physically too strenuous for him and he soon left. By this time, our paths didn't cross so much, but one evening, we had dinner together in a *charcuterie*, and he returned to his nostalgic evocations of bohemian life in Lisbon. He told me about a "girl" he'd saved from the clutches of a pimp by paying him off. His story irritated me, and I upbraided him: "You're obsessed by this idea that you're a protector and defender of hookers!" (The "girl" was nothing if not one of them, and she was just trying to exploit her generous friend.) Carlos was momentarily downcast–I had hurt him in the most sensitive area of his pride that kept him going, and had destroyed his dreams!–and he said: "You do know how to be hard and cutting sometimes!" But he ended up agreeing with me, and even bemoaned a "certain mean-spiritedness" that he had discerned in our countrymen. That same night, he suffered a violent attack of breathlessness, and in order to catch his breath he had to sit and rest on the hood of a car parked by the sidewalk. I accompanied him home, once again urging him to go and see my doctor, a specialist, and promising that I would go along with him.

But the incident had dealt a deathblow to our friendship. I too had disappointed him. If I phoned him, he showed a certain reluctance to come and see me: "One day we must meet up…" But he never showed up, and he never went to the doctor. His illness got worse, and made him irritable, more taciturn and withdrawn. He didn't even want to see his own daughter. He kept himself more and more to his own room. Another friend and his son tried to convince me that everything he told us about his past was the invention of a megalomaniac… To be honest, I had my own problems, and I found it hard to focus on a hopeless, lost cause. In my solitary walks, I would set off for Sheridan Square in the dead of night, and look up at the two windows of his apartment; they were closed and dark, or there was a faint light keeping him company in his sleeplessness. From the restaurant-nightclub, he got a daily meal delivered to him. But soon that would close, giving way to a cabaret run by Jews. I had set aside my last night in the Village to go and see him. That was when I got Agnès's call…

A few more years rushed by, and I rushed even faster until we met again. I don't recall exactly how I had heard about her divorce. I had almost forgotten that electrifying stage of my life.

Note

[1] The references are to the actress and singer, Hermínia Silva, and Portugal's most famous Fado singer, Amália Rodrigues. (Translator's note.)

Agnès–Or an Asexual Love

"Not of possession is this love made, but of caresses"

Installed provisionally in a friend's modern, luxury apartment while he was away, I was sitting in an armchair in front of the huge living-room window, under a cascade of moonlight that left everything else in shadow, when the internal phone rang and the porter informed me: "A lady to see you by the name of Agnès." I replied, startled: "Tell her to come up!" I put on my gown, went and opened the door onto the silence of the long, carpeted corridor, and waited some moments for her to appear round the far corner. Then, I ran to meet the unexpected sight of a tall, adult woman, confident and secure in her beauty. We hugged and kissed each other warmly–how long was it since we had last met? Ten years or maybe more… I couldn't believe it…

She came in and laughed: "All alone in the dark?!" I'd clean forgotten. I switched on the apartment's meager battery of lights. "I was sitting there, bathing myself in moonlight! In an old belief I have that the full moon always brings me luck. And it did; you came!" I went to the kitchen to fix some drinks–a "scotch" and a vodka–both *on the rocks*. She chose the "vodka" and said, laughing, but with passion: "I adore the moonlight! Go and switch off the lights. We can see each other and talk perfectly well without them!" I obeyed. When I returned to the living-room, I found her in the full light of the moon, stretched out on the ottoman, having thrown its numerous cushions onto the thickly carpeted floor. "What do you say to all this luxury? What a place and what a night! It's not often you get to see the stars or moonlight like this over New York! I made the right choice… But I'm no longer quite sure what brought me here. Maybe it was to re-establish a relationship with you that had never existed. Someone in the studio, apparently a friend of the owner of this apartment, mentioned your name to me, a somewhat unusual guest… I was surprised! A globe-trotter like you back here in America! What winds had brought you? I decided to come and find out. Was I wrong to do so?"–and she took a mouthful of her drink.

"It was an idea worthy of this play of light and darkness, moonlight and shadow. Only an artist such as yourself could have thought of such a thing." (For some years, she had been the chief colorist and designer for a well-known firm specializing in interior decoration, making luxury tapestries and hangings, almost all of which were done by her. She was the daughter of a Portuguese friend of mine, Carlos, now long dead.)

"An artist… you're the one who's an artist! How nice to see you again, to remember the days when father was alive and the conversations we used to have! Did you never think about seeing me again? Painting me? What do you think of me?"

"Perfection! But after you got married and your father's death, I lost track of you!"

"But you must know I got divorced, surely?"

"Yes, I was told you were colleagues, your husband a talented painter… Fiercely jealous… an alcoholic, who wanted to shut you away at home… Is that possible?!"

"Out of the question! I began a new life… or rather stayed as I was!"

Then there was silence, during which time I was able to see that her admirable, clear blue eyes were probing me with that almost hypnotic strength of old. Then, she said:

"But you never tried to court me in the way father's other friends did. Why? Didn't I please you?"

"Of course you did! Disturbingly so… But my dear girl… I'm sorry! You were eighteen to twenty years old, with an almost childlike air, and I was over fifty! Now, you're twenty-nine to thirty, isn't that so? And I'm well on my way to seventy… What could you, or can you now expect of me? Or I of you?"

"*Everything!* It was–and still is even though you are over sixty–a question of youth! Spirit! In my innocence, I once invited you alone to my apartment. You'd already been there once before to have dinner with my father, do you remember?"

"As if it were yesterday!"

"You never showed up! Didn't you understand what my intentions were?"

"In spite of my chattiness, I was always timid, and I felt anxious! Your beauty was… prohibitive!"

"That's what father said, and he told me. You never even got me to model for you, naked!"

"That would have been unthinkable! We were friends, I had your father's trust, there was the matter of your age…"

"What did that have to do with it? You never took a good look at me! Would you like to see me naked now, here in the moonlight? In fact I find it a hot night!"

I was overcome with emotion.

"I don't even dare to imagine it! And yet as an amateur sculptor and painter, I've been no stranger to the Nude, and of course nowadays…"

I finished my "scotch" and choked in my embarrassment… She cried:

"Wait!" She leapt to her feet and rushed off into a dark corner of the room. "Don't look yet!"

I turned my face away, perturbed, and sat listening to the gentle rustling of silk garments being hurriedly torn off. Then, suddenly, she reappeared in the moonlight, completely naked, like a statue of white marble, glowing and translucent! As if she both absorbed and reflected light. She reclined once more along the length of the ottoman, her right foot gently crossed over her left, her hands behind her neck underneath her loose hair, and gazed at me without moving. I could see her as clear as day: a piece of late good fortune in my old age, but an inspiring sight to behold, as if Venus or Diana had reemerged on a whim for the exclusive enjoyment of my eyes. Two virginal breasts, firm and pointed, a touch of shadow in her armpits, the gentle curve of her abdomen, the unexpected elevation of her pubis covered in a dense, black down that contrasted with her golden hair and white skin. I was excited and my heart pounded; yes, what did she expect of me? Of my near three score years and ten? That I should fall to my knees in adoration of her perfect body, symphonic in its physical beauty, and which the moonlight actually seemed to be filling with warmth? Or was I to rush over and cover her with kisses and caresses, maybe even try and make love to her? But such was her godlike serenity that I was inhibited from any idea of possession.

"Agnès, you are pure beauty!"

And she, after a brief silence, without taking her eyes off me:

"Why don't you come and fondle me? Don't you desire me? Do I frighten you?"

What I felt was something more than desire. It was boundless love. I got up from the armchair, went over and knelt down beside her, without saying a word. I stretched out my hands to touch her–wasn't this all an illusion?–to caress her, from her abundant silky hair to her calm face, where there was only a glimmer of a smile, to her neck, where her pulse beat visibly, to her chest, where I could feel her heart beating under the smoothness of her breasts, hard as fruit. It was like caressing a live statue. I felt such deep, tender feelings for her that it became almost unbearable. I stroked her abdomen with both hands, and then lay my right hand across her pubis, over its bed of crisp, curly hair–an adult female pubis on a woman who looked more like a young virgin! She lowered her hands softly over mine, and I felt her shudder slightly, as if she were telling me to stop. I remained as I was, silent and trembling, in meditation. She spoke:

"Not yet! It's too soon." And she smiled: "I remember hearing you say to my father, with your natural reserve and discretion, that 'two human beings are only joined by that which is visible.' Isn't that what you said? Do you still think so now? Don't you believe that the act of love can bring a man and a woman together in mutual revelation?"

"I still think that is the case, and what's more, that there is a conscious intimacy in this attitude of ours that cannot be discerned in the physical act of love! A sexual encounter, no matter how intimate it may be physically, is only ever vegetative. It is a progressive act, in which, once the moment of climax has been reached, we are separated from the Other by our ecstasy, so absorbed or focused are we in ourselves. There is a supreme distance in the closest union possible of the flesh!"

"Ah! How true this seemed to me then! And time confirmed it! Two beings can know each other physically, desire one another, join together and penetrate each other, quiver in mutual delight, and at the same time remain unacquainted, ignorant of the people–the souls!–enclosed within, and which make them what they are. More than once, I have made love–or what we call love–to some friend or casual acquaintance, and woken up in the early hours to gaze at the man lying next to me and, horrorstruck, thought to myself: 'Who is this stranger who chose to sleep with me?' Unaware that an act of physical possession may be desired, consented to and even enjoyed, between people who detest each other in everyday life!"

"Yes, even when it has the woman's consent, out of submissiveness, goodwill, curiosity or even desire, sex doesn't break down the barriers between two people. Take the case of dogs: how they uncouple, sad, spent, upset, merely two strangers indifferent to each other! An impersonal, natural force, like a flash of electricity during thunder, drives us towards one another, joins us, and makes us burn ardently in unison. It's like some manifestation of the "collective unconscious" of Jung, that preacher of puritanical values and the complexities of emptiness! Blind obedience to the implacable laws of life–the two cells, the gametes, that seek each other out in the darkness of the uterus to generate a new being, unknown to both!" She stopped talking for a moment, and then continued: "Only when there is a communion of feelings, ideas, tastes, experiences, opinions, is the act of love genuine: when it is the fruit of two complementary personalities or when it is possible to fuse two bodies that nature separated… Can you believe that at this precise moment, my desire for you is tantamount to pure mental exaltation?"

"Same here!" She said, laughing. "But come up here beside me!" She added, lying back a little against the wall to make room for me on the ottoman, a space I occupied without a moment's hesitation. With my arm around her shoulders, we talked in undertones, like two friends confiding in each other. "You're absolutely right! Do you know how many women–I was one of them!–feel nothing during sex? Alienated, exploited, submissive… and so often fertilized without wishing to be! The man considers himself satisfied when he has fulfilled his 'duty', and turns his back and snores, while the woman, left hungry, sleepless and, in most cases, frustrated, is resigned to bringing herself to climax with her hands! When it's not thoughtless and even brutal, the love of a man is almost always selfish. It's more often than not unimaginative, hurried, inexperienced! Full of fear! Whereas between two women who know and respect each other, who are free to choose, the union is made on the basis of consideration, sensitivity, understanding, equality, tenderness and affection, and above all give and take! It's a love that is delicate, knowledgeable, varied and uninhibited in its tactility. Nothing of the wild animal about it, a violent, painful and perhaps unwanted penetration, submission to the will of the stronger party, the male! Of course, one of them plays the tomboy's role: either because her partner chose to be submissive or because she isn't yet sufficiently liberated–in which case the affair won't last long. And if an orgasm isn't always possible–not as important as men think!–at least we are left with the feeling of some fulfillment in love. Women always enjoy the contemplation of beauty, the soft smoothness of a woman's skin. All women are to some extent beautiful! In contrast to the ape-like hide and hard musculature of many men. It's true that some women adore these signs of masculinity (or animality?) and even consider them indispensable for their attraction!" We both laughed: she in response to my perception of the woman who takes delight in my hairy, gorilla-like brothers. And she added: "While for men, erotic pleasure is generally restricted to a limited area, and rarely spreads to the whole body, for a woman, a climax is such that her whole being, every nerve, every fiber, every molecule share in a general feeling of intoxication that begins with a groan or a cry and progresses to sobs, tears, and even loss of consciousness. Sometimes it's enough for us to look at the person we desire to feel faint, or to fall into what the British call a *swoon*…But nothing compares to the feeling of mutual understanding that nature provides us with to counter pain and privation, conditions that, paradoxically, nature itself inflicts upon us!"

"That reminds me of a delightful woman I once spent time with, and to whom I complained one day about her refusal to caress me, something that I considered indispensable; she answered me: 'If a woman caressed her lover in the way that you caress me, her desire would be so violent that no man would be able to satisfy her!' By this, did she mean that only another woman could correspond to her tenderness? Passive, submissive, inactive women who lack any initiative in love, have never made me happy! The curious thing is that her greatest pleasure was being taken by surprise, while she was asleep for example, as if being taken in some primitive process of rape were the supreme form of physical possession!"

"There are pleasures," Agnès replied, "that exceed our tolerance! An old school-friend of mine told me that her husband, when their love was beginning to lose its initial ardor, had told her one day by way of a joke about the pleasures of Bilitis, and had read her bits of the poem. 'What would you do (he said) if Greta Garbo was lying here next to you instead of me?' Suddenly aroused, she hugged him close, and nervously passed her hands over his torso as if she were seeking something, and then exclaimed: 'But you haven't got anything here!' He had no breasts, he wasn't a woman… And then they made love as enthusiastically as if they were on a second honeymoon!… She was always responsive and the merest suggestion on his part drove her to ecstasy! What do you say to that?"

"Only experience shows us certain secrets! A colleague of mine married the most beautiful woman, a gifted pianist who, in spite of her being an ardent and insatiable sexual partner, confessed one day that she couldn't resist the love of her girl pupils, whom she trained in the arts of lesbianism. They were much quicker to learn these than they were the piano! He became resigned to her continuing the habit. 'You have no idea how energetic they can be!' he told me. 'It's enough to make a man terrified and die of envy! They're insatiable! Tireless! If they start making love at eleven at night, they're still going strong at daybreak!' She eventually invited him to take part in these Sapphic orgies, and he accepted out of curiosity, weakness or vice. But he ended up regretting it or growing tired and petitioned for a divorce, which caused a scandal because she contested him, using all the arguments of the loving, possessive wife that she was, in spite of her extra-marital pastimes. I asked him: 'Did you feel inferior to these women? Or were you afraid of being drawn into homosexual practices if she asked for other men to be included in the game?' At this, he bowed his head, for he couldn't answer: a sign that that was precisely what he feared, namely, that he might allow himself to be corrupted... So I advised him to leave his wife without delay and insist on never seeing her again, which is what he did–except that he only did so after visiting a well-known psychiatrist, who confirmed my verdict! He's happily married now, and a father..."

When she heard this, Agnès laughed and cuddled me passionately:

"Ah, my darling! Take me in your arms! Kiss me, caress me! Make me happy! Hearing you talk like that makes me feel you're on my wavelength, that you understand me, and by lighting my fire... you convert me!"

I hugged her as she had asked. The Moon had disappeared, leaving us in darkness. What happened then between us, or was unleashed, is beyond words. I don't know for how long we resorted to just about everything permitted by the art of love, short of my role as "male". Our sexual inhibitions were put aside. We were natural: she with her godlike body, I, despite my age, still well-toned and fit thanks to my work-outs in the gym, my rowing and running. At last she whispered: "Now that we've tried everything, my darling, to show you my gratitude, I'm going to satisfy the manly desires that I feel are being reborn in you!" And that's what was done...

Finally, she fell asleep exhausted in my arms. As for me, without knowing quite how, I followed suit. When I woke up–seated in my armchair–the Sun of a new day was shining gloriously, rising to occupy the place of the Moon that had been such a generous godmother to us. I looked around, bewildered: Agnès had vanished. There was no sign of her visit: not even a thread of hair, a used glass, a full ashtray! Even the cushions had returned to their place on the ottoman. I ran to the door; it wasn't locked, a sign that someone had left... or not! When I had greeted her, I was so excited that perhaps I had forgotten to turn the key! Might it all have been a dream, in which I had acted out subconscious desires and fantasies?

I went to look at myself in the bathroom mirror; in spite of my age, bald but without any defects, the woman had still been able to love me without feeling dominated or frustrated. What new world had I discovered—or rediscovered? Was total sexual identification and equality therefore possible? One didn't have to go that far: without sacrificing any of its natural gifts, the experience—or the dream—had just shown me what a writer of verses, whose name I've forgotten, had more or less described as follows:

... I've been everything,
all that's left for me to be is a woman!

Trading with the Enemy

Within only a few years, the office became a meeting place for our lost and dispersed folk; it was a club and somewhere to have a chat, an employment center, an office for compensation claims and an information agency. Everyone turned up there–those who had just arrived or were about to leave, those who were delivering or collecting goods or gossip, those who were trying to sell something (fruit, nuts, preserves, brandy), men who had jumped ship, and even folk engaged in a bit of harmless smuggling. They were almost always seamen. They felt better there than in government offices or in their countrymen's dingy little rooms, no better than the ones they lived in back home. An air of excitement always prevailed there, conversation and laughter echoed down the spacious marble corridors of the solid, elegant building. The surroundings gave them a certain prestige. One day, a sea-captain turned up, tearing his hair, at his wits' end: "Nearly all my men deserted me in Philadelphia! The pilot, engineer, sailors! I'm stuck... For God's sake, help me get a crew!"

Or there was the newly-arrived pilot, a young lad of good appearance, his shoulders squeezed into his tight-fitting uniform: "You see, I live with my old lady, and pay her upkeep. I don't earn enough to set up a family of my own!" The answer came as quick as a flash: "If you want to stay, we'll fix you up with a job." It wasn't that they were trying to provoke him, but temptation was a powerful thing. He thought things over for a day or two, and eventually allowed himself to be taken down to the Seamen's Union, where he registered his name. With the war, there was a shortage of crew, technicians and officers. He started off by being paid a monthly stipend. When he next turned up in the office, he was a new man; he had put on weight and radiated happiness and good health in his new, well-cut uniform made of fine cloth. "I've already sent my old lady a hundred dollars. Once things have settled down, I'll bring her over." He spoke English quite well. It wasn't long before he was made first-mate on a "Victory Ship". A few weeks later, they were hit by a torpedo in the North Atlantic and had a narrow escape. The captain was badly injured and gave him command of the ship. He acquitted himself like a veteran, was decorated for his services and promoted to the rank of captain.

"Even doctors, sir!" says Taveira. "They come here on a visit, like it, want to stay, to get a job in a hospital or in a Portuguese center… Some, in order to get residence, have contracted marriages of convenience. There are women who'll do anything, it's just a question of waving money at them! And some of them do very well. These Portuguese folk of ours are a nice bunch, it's a pleasure to help them. Poor things, they come from there embittered, and when they see they're made welcome, are respected and paid a decent wage, it's as if they get a new lease of life, a new hope in the future… And how patriotic they are! They always aspire to return home, like me, who've had thirty years of this and think of nothing else. Those days were different, and I supped with the Devil! Those who make out here, all they want to do is bring their relatives over, their friends, folk from home, just so as to see them made happy, too. Our people have a good heart, good ideals! The down side is our feeling of being so alone and so insignificant! But no matter how much a man gets used to this, it's there that we want to return to end our days. There's no homeland like ours. The climate, the sunshine, the kindly people, the tasty food…"

The reception in honor of the Latin American union leaders, in the penthouse of the T… Hotel was proceeding in formal but animated fashion. Apart from numerous North Americans, there were representatives of the British Labor Party. All for the sacred Allied cause. With a "high-ball" in my hand, I was among a group of people talking on the terrace, when a jovial "playboy", doing the rounds, came up to me. His dress was casual but impeccable, and his English was that of a genuine Oxford "fellow":

"Chilean, am I right?"

"No, Portuguese."

"Portuguese! I'm delighted to hear it. I should have guessed. We're old friends, allies!"–He told me his name (which I didn't catch) and added: "British Vice-Consul. Would you have a moment?"–And he took me by the arm.

"Of course."

Photographers flashed their bulbs, taking picture after picture. We stood there together, arm in arm, like old friends and allies, with idiotic smiles. I'm already a marked man. This sudden friendship… What does he want from me? Or can it be…?

"I adore the Portuguese. I served in Lisbon for two years!"

We exchanged banalities, and then, suddenly, he said:

"So you must know Tavério, a compatriot of yours?"

"Taveira? He's an American citizen. We're good friends."

"Ah! In that case maybe you can tell me…"

The speeches were beginning in the reception room. We were separated by a sudden rush of guests. Freed from my interrogator, I went and sat down alone, in an almost empty row of chairs. When my wife arrived soon afterwards, I said:

"There's an Englishman following me around. He's after something. As soon as this finishes, let's get out of here. Let's head straight for the elevators…"

Almost at the same moment, a jovial voice addressed me on my left:

"What a coincidence! We meet again."

The guy's a fool. Or he takes me for one. He wants to talk some more. It annoyed me, and I didn't even listen to the speeches, which in any case were unnecessary: friendship and inter-American solidarity, the usual platitudes. My wife had already grasped the situation.

At the first opportunity, we sneaked off. We were getting into the elevator and suddenly, there was someone running after us: "One moment!" And there he was getting in too.

"That was a bit of luck!" and then, hurriedly, given that time was against him: "You must know another compatriot of yours, Mr. DelNegro?"

"So-so. Why?"

The lift stopped, took on more people, and continued its descent, packed solid.

"Apparently, he does business with the Germans!" said the playboy, crushed to the point of asphyxiation.

"Is that so? I don't know. Portugal's neutral, isn't it? Or at least, that's what you people want it to be."

"But it's our ally! And we're at war with Germany! What's more, he's a Jew. DelNegro. Don't you find it strange?"

I burst out laughing. We reached the foyer. There I stopped:

"If you want to hamper trade with the Germans, why don't you go and try it? It might be easier than you think…"

The vice-consul took a step back, smiled, lifted his arm, and as he twirled his little felt hat on the tip of a finger, exclaimed:

"Now you've scored a point!… 'Bye!" and he disappeared into the gathering darkness.

The bird had flown. Annoying. But he left me feeling uncomfortable. DelNegro, worldly and debonair, had admitted to me with childish imprudence that he had secret business dealings with Germany, I don't know what in. And so what? What business was it of mine? I don't stick my nose in other people's affairs. The one who gave me cause for concern was Taveira, a sincere, generous man who was a friend of good causes–and a friend of mine. On more than a dozen occasions, I had been visited by agents from various branches of the secret service, including a senior official from the State Department. What a great honor! They all wanted to know things: sometimes about myself (some kind countrymen of mine, either naïve or malicious, but in any case anxious to show they were rubbing shoulders with the great and the good, gave me the cold shoulder), sometimes about vague generalities, or even to find out about people they thought were acting suspiciously (and who might not have been). What did they suspect? It even crossed my mind they might be warning me… On the advice of more experienced friends, I always greeted them politely, just as they in fact treated me. But I knew so little! Always wrapped up in my work… Faces? Names? I knew almost no one! And as for generals! I'd never had truck with anyone above the rank of lieutenant. I hadn't even ever seen one at close quarters. Leaders? Of what? I've been an expatriate for some years now, and things have changed so much over there! Apart from that, allied censors (in particular the British) were in the habit of intercepting or withholding my correspondence, books and newspapers. And as for business, I don't understand the first thing about it. I've heard (via the bigwig from the State Department, silk lapels and white flashings on his waistcoat, who had a machine hidden in his desk recording our conversation) that their lordships have some twelve hundred diplomatic functionaries on active service; they must have much greater and better knowledge than I have (the man laughed).

They weren't going to get anything from here. At least not as far as

I was aware. Hell is full of good intentions.

The agents from the Treasury, hats on their head, hands in pockets and feet up on the table where they had spread the accounts books, had been grilling Taveira for two hours. They wanted to know to whom he had sold the platinum.

"I've no idea who he was! I was alone here at lunchtime, between twelve and one, when I saw his outline, standing there reading my name on the glass panel of the door. He came in without knocking: Mister Taveira? You're speaking to him. He didn't sit down or even take his hat off. I thought he might be from the Government, too! Did I sell fine metals? I haven't got any in stock, but I can get some. He stood there a while looking at me: I need some platinum. It's for my own use, a delicate piece of apparatus. Are there any restrictions? And I answer: not at the moment, as long as it's for the domestic market. If it's for export, the Government will want to know where it's going. How much can you get for me? It depends. How much do you need? It was a reasonable amount. If you want to drop by here later this afternoon, or if you give me a call, I'll give you an answer right away. I've got to consult my suppliers. Is four o'clock convenient? I'll be here at four. And off he went. I didn't even remember to ask him his name."

"Had you never seen him before?"

"Never. I phoned Watts & Co., on William Street. Have you got any platinum? As much as you want. It's not for export, is it? No sir, it's for a domestic client. Okay, be here at eleven o'clock tomorrow. When the man phoned, it wasn't even four yet, and I gave him an answer. And I asked for his name and address: J. Felinsky, 698 Kelly Street, Palmerston, New Jersey. I've still got the note I took of it, here, you can see for yourselves. Come by here tomorrow at one in the afternoon, and bring the money. I'll be there at one without fail."

"He came, paid in cash: you won't find me taking a check from a stranger! Or even asking for identification. It's not the custom to ask indiscreet questions. My job is buying and selling. If I've got it, I'll sell it; if I haven't got it, I send them somewhere else. I take my commission and that's it. And you know something? Without even getting off my butt, between two phone calls I've even managed to make a hundred percent profit. Is that immoral? I think so, too. But it's war, and I'm not the one who invented this system. The obstacles and formalities are enough as it is—licenses, quotas, restrictions, cargo space, insurance, exchange rates; it's hell. And my taxes are all paid up."

"That's what remains to be found out."

The next day, there they were again:

"Tavey, you gave us a false address. 698 doesn't exist, it's an empty lot, full of trash. And there's no Felinsky there. You made him up."

"What do you mean made him up?! That was the name he gave me. I've never lied in my life."

"Okay, but there's always a first time. You're exporting platinum on the quiet. That's called trading with the enemy."

"With the enemy?! So are we at war? Not to my knowledge. And I don't even sell abroad."

"If we catch you at it, at the very least we'll close your joint down. If someone puts the word in…"

"You guys know better than I do how things work. The high and mighty export as much platinum as they want, millions and millions of dollars, and no one bats an eyelid. They send it to Greece, where the Germans pick it up by plane. The government looks the other way. They grease the palm of whoever they need to! But we small-fry can't even sell an ounce. Do you call that equality, democracy? There can't be one law for the rich and another for the poor! I know my rights. As long as it's not prohibited, I'll go on selling it. I don't know where it's going."

"Tavey, don't pass judgment, and don't provide false witnesses. Keep your nose clean and do your duty. We'll do ours. If you cooperate with us and tell us who you sold it to, we'll leave you alone."

"You've got the books there, the deposit slips and check stubs, all the correspondence. Investigate. Have fun!"

He laughed as he told me this, and added:

"They want to show their bosses how conscientious they are. They've been following me around for weeks. Even yesterday they were picking my brains all afternoon. Every tiny amount, even the crossings out in the books, they want an explanation for everything. Let them call in the book-keeper! It even crossed my mind they might be after a backhander. But this is small-time business… They're making my life hell. They even wanted to know all about the story of the banknotes."

"The story of the banknotes!"–Tiago, who has worked closely with him, says to me–"I can tell you about that. The guy's done well for himself. He's a cunning one, not to be trusted. Just imagine, some time ago I made him a business proposal; we'd go in as equal partners, half and half: This isn't going to make any money, it's worthless! So I pulled out. A few days later, he does a deal and makes a packet! Do you see what I mean, pal? When I gave him a piece of my mind, do you know what he answered? That business and friendship are like oil and vinegar: they never mix well. That business is all about double-dealing, seeing who can slit the next man's throat first!"

"Well, at least lets salvage friendship. Idealism! That's not to be sniffed at."

"It was he who thought up this business of the banknotes. It was such a simple idea!"

"It's the simple ideas that are difficult to get to the bottom of: Columbus's egg, the king in his birthday suit... They're the ones that make the world go round. But tell me about it."

"Well, now, lets see. With the influx of refugees into Portugal, their sights set on shipping out to America, it was a gift. Many of them, their shoes worn down and patched up, carried suitcases full of gold, coins, precious stones. And dollars by the fistful. Coffers were being emptied all over Europe. Those who had to stay longer in Portugal—some even had to wait for years—had to change their money and spend it. The market was saturated, ships were being torpedoed, there was a lack of transport, it was difficult to send money abroad, and many currency changers couldn't get rid of their money. The dollar note fell in value, and at one point was worth just twelve escudos. This at a time when the dollar check was worth twenty-nine! What the commercial sector needed were checks drawn on America. But where were they? The government doesn't want any more notes here: fear of inflation, or that Europe won't have the means to exchange them, goodness knows. So what did he come up with? Well, good old Treasury notes, who's going to stop me having and using them? It was as simple as that! He issued an instruction to his agent in Lisbon: Buy as many dollars as you can! And that's what he's gone on doing. Some days, there isn't a dollar to be found on the market. There are lads in the merchant navy, good folk I feel sorry for, who are desperate to make a bit of money. They bring him notes and charge ten percent for carrying them. That's not at all bad! He goes to the bank and exchanges them for checks drawn on the New York money market. He dispatches them on to Lisbon, where they're worth twice as much or more! Do you get it? That's what they want over there. Ninety to a hundred percent guaranteed profit. It's for those in the know, he says."

"Now, with the American landings, I'll tell you something else: we've had another flood of money. Occupation dollars, that's what they call them. Haven't you seen them? Look, I've got one here. Just like the normal ones, except that the seal is a different color. With the GIs spending them like water!... It's a good time to buy occupation dollars. The government doesn't want them here, but soldiers send them to their families, or bring them back... No bank refuses to accept them... You've no idea what a smuggling racket there is. It's enabled a lot of people to escape poverty. I just wish I'd done the same; I'd be rich!"

(But he never explained how he'd got hold of that occupation dollar note).

And it's not just Taveira. Oh, no. From time to time, the dock police catch a seaman with banknotes and confiscate them; they always claim they're going shopping. They come ashore at night and have adopted the habit of carrying them tied up in a handkerchief. If they see a Fed coming, they throw the packet under a car or truck parked along the side of the street, and then after they've been frisked, they go back and pick it up. There's a bit of a risk, but it's worth it; a hundred dollars can be as much as two or three months' wages. One of them was so inspired, he tied the packet to his little finger with some black cotton thread, just in case someone tried to steal it or he lost it in the darkness. When the agents told him to raise his arms, he obeyed and tossed the packet up and over. They didn't find anything in his pockets. But then one of them touched the thread with his hand–"What's this?" he pulled it in slowly, and along came the packet: "Aha! We've got some banknotes here! Don't you know this is against the law?" With the fright he got, or maybe it was out of cunning, the seaman had a funny turn and ended up in a lunatic asylum. Not long afterwards, he was deported back home at the Consulate's expense: and carrying his notes with him of course. They always return them. Taveira says:

"They're not as bad as they're made out to be. The FBI boys!"

"Unless they're pretending to be blind so as to catch us red-handed!"

He gazed at me, his eye half-closed because of the smoke from his Cuban cigar:

"I've thought of all that too!" he took his La Caza from his mouth, looked at it and smiled. "This little cigar tastes so good! Some nights I sit here like this till late, smoking in the darkness and mulling over some business venture. I love this game. I was born for it, I don't want any other life!"

The seaman brings me messages from my family and friends, books and other items I ask him to get.

"As far as I can see, you're involved in this banknote 'racket' too. Isn't that dangerous?"

"There's nothing I can do about it. What I earn isn't enough to live on! I've got a couple of clients over here. Their agents deal with everything over there in Lisbon. I don't have to lift a finger; it's just a question of going along to the office and picking up the notes. I've even brought thousands over at a time. Almost all of it for the firm. It's a heavy responsibility, and some nights I can't sleep! I'm afraid it'll be stolen, and what's worse, on board ship…"

He's as skinny and wizened as a shad, from all the tasks he has to carry out. He rushes around looking for the things people have asked him to buy. He goes back to Lisbon loaded with drugs, medicine, sulfates, vitamins, nylon stockings, shirts, and goodness knows what else. (Later, there'd be that stuff I heard one of them refer to as "peninsulin", and car tires. A whole way of life. The Portuguese have learnt to pass through the finest mesh in the network of formalities and restrictions that have crushed them for centuries. The mighty and the meek!)

"And haven't you ever run into trouble either here or over there?"

"Nah! I've got my connections. And then these folk here go crazy over Portuguese brandy. I give them a little bottle… Listen to this story because it's funny. But keep it to yourself! Some months ago, I was carrying ten thousand dollars for the firm, when in the middle of the crossing we get a radio message from Lisbon: no cargo Baltimore proceed New Orleans await orders. We change course. What a pretty state of affairs! So off I go to New Orleans carrying all my stuff! If something happens, a robbery or illness… When we get there, I wire New York: not going Baltimore order delivered next voyage. One afternoon, I go and have a meal in a bar and meet a fellow who tells me that in Mexico, all you have to do is go into a bank with dollars and ask for gold; they'll exchange each one for "aztecas" worth twenty pesos; this size! Fine quality gold you can bend with your fingers! I couldn't sit still. I was determined to get down to Mexico myself to exchange my notes! I went back to the ship and was so excited that even the captain asked me whether I had a touch of fever. A fever indeed! Not unless it's a gold fever… Anyway, I tell him the story, and ask whether he'll let me nip over to Vera Cruz by plane, two, three days at the most. After all, the ship's going to be held up in New Orleans. Okay, pal, he says, but make it quick. And for God's sake, lend me a few dollars because I've got no cash at all. I'll pay you fifteen percent interest, and commission on top of that! He was so persistent that there was nothing else I could do but promise to buy a few "aztecas" on his account. A few titbits I lost out on, but then life at sea means we have to look after each other. And when it's the captain, well… But you can see the risk, if the Americans get suspicious, if they search me and take the gold? Here in America, it's forbidden to have gold! He says to me: leave that to me, I'll take responsibility for it. I'll have a word with the consul who's a friend of mine. So off I go to Vera

Cruz scared out of my wits. I didn't sleep a wink for two whole nights. I exchanged the dollars I had with me for "aztecas", including the ten thousand for the firm. I returned loaded, you just can't imagine. Nothing happened to me, and the captain, poor fellow, even made a fair amount. I've never had such a good journey. The following voyage, when we returned to Baltimore, I came up to New York and gave Taveira his banknotes. And this is what he says to me: so you make a whole pile of money with my dollars, and you don't even offer me a tip? (How did he know I'd gone to Mexico to buy gold? There are no secrets among our folk!) Well, what more do you want? Here's your money, what does it matter to you where it's been? And he even paid me the ten percent commission, so he did. That's to show him he's not the only smart one!"

(To be frank, my admiration for our people's ingenuity knows no bounds.)

"Why, sir, don't you (he was talking to me now) make a bit on the side too? You kill yourself working, slaving over your books! It would help a bit. I'll arrange everything for you. You don't have to lift a finger, don't pay me anything up front, don't even pay me for carriage. I'll deliver your banknotes and that's it."

"Me? Don't even think of it. It's not that I think it's a crime; I'm against any form of restriction. But unlike Cesar's wife, it's not enough for me to appear honest. I've got to be honest, too. One day soon, it will all come into the open… Someone must deprive himself for the love of principles."

The man must have thought me a bit of a simpleton, or an idiot. An Idealist! When he returned from Lisbon, he handed me a hundred dollars: "It's your profit" he said. "How come?" "I pretended you were my partner for a hundred dollars, do you understand?" I didn't understand, and he explained patiently: "Over there, I bought a thousand dollars in banknotes with the money I had, some fourteen thousand escudos. I credited you with a hundred. Instead of the fifteen thousand escudos that would have given me the check for a thousand, I only earn just over twelve. The rest is yours. Now do you understand?" I spent two days thinking about it, but I doubt whether I understood. This lad had struggled to get his third grade at high school and had always failed his math. And the ones who rule the world are graduates, as Taveira says! Anyhow, he gave me a hundred dollars for free; I'm not made of wood and I accept the tip. (They owe me a good few favors too!) When I spoke to Taveira about this with some reservations, his comment was:

"That thief's as sharp as a fox. He'll make a fortune, you'll see!"

"Good luck to him. He's worked hard enough for it."

Not the least complaint. He was not lacking in a sense of justice.

"Drop by!" he says to me over the phone. "There's someone here who wants to meet you." I never turned down his invitations. I went along. It was Captain Craveiro, a short, energetic man, jolly and ruddy-faced, with the greenest little eyes. A charming man. We talked.

"Well, I've been doing this for over forty years. I cut my teeth making my living on the sea. Now I'm old, or no longer merit their confidence: they've withdrawn my master's ticket and demoted me to first mate, from horse to donkey. I've got a daughter who is no longer young and never had enough money to get herself a husband. I never made a cent from business, my business was always sailing the seas. And how many people I watched making fortunes! It's not that I envied them; but quite frankly, to live and die in poverty! What can a man do? Tell me honestly: what's the point of being honorable? All you get is a kick in the you-know-what and have a nice day! I'm just sorry I didn't learn sooner. Now I'm too old to stay here; this is a good place to be young…"

I realized they had other matters to discuss and I left. His ship was moored at a wharf on the East River, in New York. Some days later, Taveira phoned again: "Come and have lunch with us. The captain was delighted to meet you. He's leaving today and he'd like to say goodbye."

We met in a dockside bar full of people, smoke, and a clamor in half a dozen languages. The food was good, Mediterranean, like our own. Things that are gradually dying out, demolished along with the poetry of the seaports of old. We ate and drank in moderation, we talked and laughed. Craveiro was jubilant!

"I shan't be coming back here again. This is my last voyage. I'm giving up life on the sea, and it's about time. Thanks to our friend here. I've taken stock of my life; I'm going to retire and open a tobacconist's… You'll see; I'll still get my daughter married off!" He looked at his watch: "Okay, I'd better go aboard. We cast off at six. Come and see me over there."

"We'll meet up again in the old country."

He left and started to pick his way across the road, which was wide and busy at that point. It was as if he feared being run over. He was limping.

"What the hell's wrong with him? Has he got rheumatism in his legs? The other day he was walking along like a young lad of twenty, he even looked as if he was dancing. And now he's lame?"

Taveira laughed, and nudging me in the ribs, he took his cigar out of his mouth and said in an undertone:

"Rheumatism my foot! That's from the goods. He's carrying his pension in his shoes! A small fortune in platinum…"

We stood there silently until we saw him disappear inside the huge hangar. Then I turned to Taveira, who was smiling, his eyes moist. Grateful, I put my arm tenderly round his shoulders. It doesn't matter to me that he's made a small fortune, or that he's a "trickster" and "untrustworthy"! Or that they accuse him of smuggling! Envy him as much as you like, for there's plenty there to envy. It's not just for money that he lives and works. There's something else in him beyond the thirst for profit–a sense of human warmth, fellow-feeling, an urge to be charitable and to do good, to help others out of hardship, to alleviate, in so far as this is possible, life's misfortunes and inequalities. Dear, good Taveira. He's an institution I'm proud of.

We turned on our heels and began to walk.

"So what about the Treasury boys? Are they still taxing your patience?"

"They won't leave me alone. They want to know who I'm selling the platinum to. They're determined to get their hands on it but not if I can prevent it."

Could it be that they believed his explanations? Or did they turn a blind eye too? Why weren't they there on the quay, watching him?

I had some tasks to do that afternoon and couldn't go aboard. I never saw the affable sailor again.

This Spaniard has been phoning me for days, citing the names of friends and acquaintances of mine in order to get me to meet him. I thought he sounded suspicious, and I asked someone to tell me about him: "Be careful, for that one's a traitor, a man who's sold his soul! One of the so-called 'three letters'–the FBI!" Eventually, he caught me unawares in the office one afternoon. I told him to come in.

"Have you brought the letter of introduction?"

"No, but I can phone them…"

"You're not phoning anyone. Are you so bad-mannered that you can turn up here without the introduction you promised? Who sent you here?"

What a fitting welcome! I was sick of receiving "visitors", and decided to be bad-mannered myself. In English, which he spoke badly. He was confused, almost in tears. He'd fought on the Republican side, was now in difficulties, with a weak lung and a family to support… (I know that story only too well!) He had eventually taken his current job–informer. His confession was as repellent as it was uncalled for.

"If you help me, I can give you all the information you want!"

"A cop story, espionage, exchange of information, that's it, isn't it? Well, I don't fall for that type of scheme. And as for the little you know, I'm not interested, nor is what I know, which is nothing, of any interest to your bosses. Leave me alone and go and see to your own health."

He leaned towards me, and I noticed that his cheap shirt had a tear next to the collar. The wretched creature didn't even earn enough for a decent shirt. I took pity on him and allowed him to make his point: that the question he wanted to ask didn't compromise me in any way, I had his word for it. It just concerned the Jew, DelNegro, and Taveira. That was all!

"The authorities are convinced that Taveira's office is a den of smugglers: business deals involving platinum, currency exchange, trading with the enemy! You understand: we are all opposed to Fascism! And now we're at war with the Third Reich! It's all for the Cause!..." He pleaded, clutching at straws so as not to drown. I had to laugh:

"So the FBI and Mr. Hoover are against Fascism too? Well let me make myself perfectly clear: this man Taveira, whom they want to catch and get rid of, is the most honorable and loyal man I have ever known; he would give the shirt off his back to the poor, to the persecuted, to an unfortunate wretch like yourself! And he's already done so. He's a man of principles. With so many bandits growing rich on the backs of millions of dead, out of disasters and ruination, is that what you call serving the Cause? Go and tell that to your bosses if you have a shred of courage or shame. Oh yes! That is certainly trading with the enemy."

I don't remember ever having been so rude to anyone. I didn't even think of the consequences. The poor fellow quite literally stumbled out of the room. But there were no more visits after that, curious, isn't it? Nor, as far as I know, did they trouble Taveira again, Taveira who only thinks of packing his bags and returning once and for all to Portugal, his dream. The day he leaves, this place won't be the same; it'll be the end of an era. Those who come later (they are already arriving) won't have known the bitter hardship, the sacrifices, the fervor, novelty and strangeness of all this. Nor will they experience the incurable nostalgia for that which never happened.

And to be honest, these newcomers no longer interest me.

The Bow Tie

The receptionist rang through to my desk and said: " Mr. Ribeiro Couto is here to see you."[1] This Anglo-American "see" is what we mean by "paying one's respects" or "visiting". I turned excitedly to my colleague on the editorial team of the *International Review of Chewing-Gum* and said: "It's Ribeiro Couto; he's come to visit me!" He almost leapt up, exclaiming: "Take care, he's a dangerous fellow! He's a mulatto, a fascist, one of Plínio Salgado's green shirts! They used to call him 'the green-eyed *mulata* from Santos'!"

"It doesn't matter. Green eyes, green shirt–maybe a combination of different colors, no? And as for 'mulatto', who isn't one nowadays? Anyway, I have a great deal of respect for him. And from what I've read of his, I haven't seen anything fascist in it."

This same colleague, who later would become the high priest of Brazil's literary bureaucracy, had once given me a detailed description of the "mulattoes", a hateful word: "white mulatto", the one who has a white man's face and the soul of a mulatto, or a subservient black; he is deceitful, bitter, prone to intrigue (Ribeiro Couto would be one of those!); and "mulatto white", one who is dark-skinned, but considers himself white and behaves like one. And in Brazil, he was prone to say, there's no racial discrimination. Only a deep respect for the various shades of color among human beings, in "the world that the Portuguese made" and outside it as well, prevented me from replying: "And which of the two orders do you belong to?"

I was not personally acquainted with Ribeiro Couto, whose work had first been revealed to me by that faithful lover of literature, José Osório de Oliveira. Years after the publication of my book, *Páscoa Feliz*, when I was already in New York, I had received from him an enthusiastic dedicatory message in his little volume, *Correspondência de Família*, two letters in verse exchanged between him and Casais Monteiro, who had given him my novel to read. I didn't reply or thank him because of my old habit of waiting for the moment of Total Inspiration (which never comes) before replying to literary letters (which I hate) or thanking an author for sending me a book, with the result that I never get round to it. And what a fool I felt! Should I perhaps take the opportunity to apologize?...

I told the receptionist to send him in. The moment he arrived in the office, with its glass front, which made us look like pets in a cage, Ribeiro Couto came over to me, as I stood there waiting somewhat shamefully, and hugged me cordially:

"You ungrateful Portuguese who doesn't answer his admirers' letters!"

As his compatriot (who moments before had tried to turn me against him) was getting up from his desk, maybe in the hope of also receiving a hug, the poet, still clutching me to his chest, turned to him:

"As for you, you no-good Bahian, I don't even want to shake your hand!"

The other went green and yellow and didn't say a word. He was the sort who kept his thoughts to himself until a chance arose: let's say he was the subservient type! Although put out, I admired Ribeiro Couto's honesty, the exact opposite of the supposed deceitfulness of the "white-mulatto". I noticed that he was dressed soberly but with careless elegance, the absent-minded air of a writer-diplomat and cosmopolitan man of the world; he wore a tweed jacket, with a button missing as if to accentuate his stylishness, and flannel trousers.

"Shall we go and have lunch at the *Bistro* on Third Avenue? I'm inviting you." (This was directed at me).

We were on our way out when my colleague hurried after us:

"I'm coming with you!"

Ribeiro Couto stopped and turned:

"I didn't invite you, you Bahian....!"

Even so, he came along with us. You have to be pretty hard-nosed. Was it that he didn't want to miss our memorable conversation, or that he feared we might talk about him behind his back?

During lunch at the *Bistro*, he remained quiet. At a certain point in our lively chatter, Ribeiro Couto looked at me, and suddenly said:

"But Miguéis, how Americanized you are!"

I felt the color draining from my face, and put my fork down:

"How do you mean? I don't understand."

"You're eating with your left hand hidden in your lap, just as Emily Post tells you to do in her *Manual of Etiquette*!"

Whatever it was I was eating, and I think it was *paté de foie-gras*, didn't require the use of a knife, and I was holding a fork in my right hand without a thought for what my left hand was doing. At the same time, I had never even paged through Emily Post's manual, one of the most popular books in the United States after the Bible, of course, and more so than *Gone with the Wind*, and more recently, Dr Spock's *Baby and Child Care*. The remark cut me to the quick. For some moments I was unable to swallow my *paté*. Then at last, I said:

"I wasn't even aware of what I was doing."

Then, in a gradual, gentle explosion, I thought to myself: "My good friend, if instead of a highly paid diplomat and a respected author, you had come to live here out of love for an idea or some thing, to earn your hard crust of exile like me, in freedom and obscurity, maybe you would also be forced to eat cheap meals at the counter of coffee-shops round here, democratically squeezed between a truck driver and a black window cleaner. In such a situation, and in the absence of vital space, you'd get used to eating with your left hand hidden in your lap. Even without ever having read the Manual of Etiquette!"

But could it be that he had understood? Can those who are privileged with good luck or fortune ever understand the language of those who aren't? It's the habit that makes the monk... My admiration for the poet and writer was too great for me to feel any rancor. At the same time, it was the modern figure of Fradique Mendes who was sitting there, an archetype of Latin American social position, whether white or mestizo, and it was the prototype that irritated me, not the individual person.

I limited myself to saying:

"Talking of Americanization, let me tell you what I heard one day from a compatriot and a colleague of yours, talking about another Brazilian. It went something like this: 'This fellow has become completely Americanized. Can't you see he's wearing a bow-tie and a jacket with a slit at the back?' He who doesn't use the same feather in his headdress as I do isn't my type. That's the stuff of the most oppressive form of tribalism…"

(In fact, the bow-tie is far more European than American.)

Ribeiro Couto's hand went to his bow-tie. Then I remembered that his elegant tweed jacket had a slit at the back… Without wishing to, I had touched on an inconvenient subject, entirely inappropriate among diplomats, though common among men of letters less given to prejudice. And hadn't he been brutally frank with his compatriot and my colleague, who was there with us? (And who no doubt was now laughing at our expense!) Brazilians, in their immense cordiality, treat each other with a frankness that I greatly envy.

Lunch ended and I didn't see Ribeiro Couto again. We didn't exchange "family correspondence", or anything else, although I continued to follow his brilliant career, as best I could, from afar. Over twenty years later, I mourned his death in Paris, a solitary dandy and prince among Brazilian short story writers.

But don't come and ask me what hidden intentions today caused me to evoke the incident.

Note

[1] Ribeiro Couto (1898-1963) was a Brazilian poet and fiction writer associated with the Modernist Movement launched in 1922. He worked for the Brazilian diplomatic service between 1929 and 1952. (Translator's note.)

Holiday

The day (a weekday) was warm and tranquil, the place deserted, the sun filtered from a uniformly silver sky, the water like a mirror and almost completely still: "Shall we go for a trip?" They stepped out of the "Olds"—ten years of use, two hundred dollars third or fourth hand—and he went over to the hut with its sign "Boats for hire", and paid for one. Without saying a word, the man handed him the ticket with the time on it, eleven twenty a.m. He chose a long, low skiff, of solid appearance, with four oars. "I only need two." The man took in the second pair. His wife and daughter sat in the stern. He, wearing a short-sleeved shirt, sat down more towards the bow, placed his feet on the slat and fitted the oars into the steel rowlocks. Crouching on the pontoon, the man pushed the boat out from the landing stage, walked back to his hut, still without saying a word, and disappeared.

They were alone. Over the hut, turned to the landward side, there was a sign mounted on two metal poles. He hadn't noticed it. What could it say? Some advertisement for fishing tackle. He rowed slowly and steadily out into the middle of the lake. The water was absolutely smooth, reflecting the colorless sky and the light from the invisible sun. He looked along the shore; it was low, without any variation or elevation, except for some occasional clumps of trees. In the middle of the lake he paused for a moment and then made for the headwaters, some hundreds of meters to the north. There, they stopped for a while in the shade of some branches, next to the clear, sluggish stream that flowed out between moss and grass and fed the lake.

It was good to be there listening to the babbling waters. Apart from this, silence oozed from the sky through the web of leaves and spread over the surface of the lake. From time to time, a trout would leap out of the water into the air to catch some insect, a dragonfly hovering over the stream like a tiny airplane on patrol, before falling back into the water, always with the same plop. He wasn't a fisherman; he liked them alive, or otherwise, grilled with melted butter, lemon and parsley. He thought about lunch, which they would have round about one o'clock in a *lunch-room* somewhere by the roadside. Starlings and blackbirds rustled among the trees, played or tussled together on the grass, fighting over grubs and worms. They drew themselves up high in their efforts to pull their elastic bodies out of the ground, and some even fell over backwards comically. The mother spoke quietly to her little girl, who was pointing to things and asking questions. He looked at them and smiled. They hadn't had such fun for a long time. The atmosphere was one of a holiday, long yearned for and heartily deserved.

He then rowed slowly in a zigzag for about an hour, crossing the lake from shore to shore, skillfully managing the oars in opposite directions so as to make the boat turn like a top—and they would laugh giddily. It was relaxed, monotonous and restful. Happiness was this scarcely imagined peace, this interval between the struggles and displeasure of earning a living. He felt vigorous in his skinny frame, a bundle of nerves, which sometimes hurt him as if they had been exposed. He took deep breaths of still air, which was cool for a summer's day. The rhythm, the effort and the atmosphere placated his anxieties. He tried rowing fast. The skiff, light and well balanced, glided like a skate, brushing over the water, leaving only the slightest wake, which was soon diluted and reabsorbed into the water.

"Shall we go to the other end?" He went swiftly straight back to the middle, and then rowed down the lake. The hut was left far behind to his left. Looking behind over his right shoulder, he noticed, still some distance away, a dark, low building on some rocks, like a small tower: some abandoned dwelling, a factory or a mill. There wasn't any sign of industrial activity in the place. A light breeze was now blowing, ruffling the lake with little waves that hurried along with the boat. It was only then that he noticed the current that was helping him along. The lake must have been deeper at this point. Or was it the tide? A little freshwater lake, far from the sea, doesn't have tides. Or could it have? He continued to row effortlessly, with his back to it.

He looked again, this time over his left shoulder. On the opposite side of the lake to the little tower, he caught sight of a large shed that scarcely showed above the terrain. The only limit between the two buildings was the waterline: some hundred and eighty to two hundred meters wide. The lake came to an end there, but what was strange was the absence of any sign of a shore, rocks or any other obstacles. Only further away, beyond this line, could he see trees and vegetation. He rowed faster as if trying to reach his target. The skiff slid along, quivering slightly, with a muffled gurgling sound as if it had scraped the bottom. The current pulled it forward. The breeze dropped, the water was once more smooth and mirror-like, thick and uniform. He looked at the tower again, which was now much nearer; it had the air of an old factory, possibly for making cotton goods or paper, or of an abandoned mill. In this land, everything grows, passes its prime and disappears quickly. A good place to spend one's holidays perhaps. The skiff seemed to be moving weightlessly, almost flying over the surface of the water.

He found this strange. He stopped rowing and drew in the oars, slightly alarmed by the feeling that the water was getting thicker, and moving forward more concertedly. It seemed to be growing or its level rising, and there was now a metallic, electric glimmer from the sun on its surface; it was gathering speed. Was it my imagination? He couldn't see any reason for the current: a rare, insidious, hidden force that was dragging them forward.

Suddenly, the woman, her face grown pale, punctuated the silence with a brief scream and grabbed her daughter, whose eyes were round with terror, clutching her to her breast. He glanced behind him; they were not far from the edge, and the water suddenly disappeared, glinting perversely. He then realized that it was getting thicker and rising in order to break through the invisible barrier. They were being carried towards a weir or a precipice. There was no time to lose. Aware of the danger and without speaking, he tried to slow and halt the boat's advance by jamming the oars into the water against the current; but it propelled them irresistibly forward, bending the oars and threatening to tear them from his hands. He began to row backwards with unexpected vigor, so as to force the boat to change course, aware at the same time of the danger of capsizing... Even so he didn't let up. It was a waste of time to start thinking! They were five or six meters from the weir—it was, indeed, a weir!—from falling over, maybe from... He heard the crash of the waters and imagined the rest.

With a frantic effort—*Save our lives!* —drawing himself up, with his feet firmly planted on the wooden slat, he at last succeeded in forcing the skiff to do a one hundred and eighty degree turn, so that its bow was turned toward the headwaters of the lake, which were invisible from there. The woman, silent, hugged the little girl, shielding her eyes. There wasn't a sound in the peaceful air, apart from the sinister thunder of the weir nearby. Having started to pull away, he concentrated all his strength in his wrists and rowed like a desperado to escape from the horrendous power of suction, against the clearly hostile current, foaming with rage and scorn around the bow of the boat, which offered it less grip than the stern only a few moments before. The water had a hard, dull sheen that came from the sky, and had an almost animal consciousness, obstinately intent on murder. But amid that natural solitude, he also felt a strange delight in combat, in confronting the enemy... Breathless and covered in sweat, in a few minutes he had got them out of danger.

He rowed towards the shore. He looked back again at the line of the weir, which was now receding into the distance, and heaved a sigh of relief. The water was once again serene, as if at peace with itself. Humanized and submissive, it had lost that ill-omened glitter, and lapped against the bow, rhythmically tapping the base of the boat, which had not taken in so much as a drop of water. Satisfied, he relaxed and rowed at a leisurely pace past the reeds along the shore. They hadn't exchanged a word.

When they reached the landing stage, he tied up, helped his wife and daughter out, and leapt onto dry land. The man, his pipe between his teeth, came down to meet them. "Why didn't you warn us? Who would have guessed there was a weir? We were almost washed over it." The man shrugged his shoulders and pointed at the sign with his pipe: *Boating at your own risk...* Not a word of warning. He paid the man for the one and three quarter hours, and he went back into his hut without saying a word. *Bob the Silent One!* It's no use, that's the way this country is. When they don't talk too much! Just imagine if there's an accident... Oh! They'll do the deal first for sure. Yes, indeed, once the house has been robbed...

Feeling angry–the incident was spoiling his holiday, his outing, his happiness–he drove for some time down the tarred road that followed at some distance the shore of the lake. Near the narrow end of this, he stopped and got out with his wife to take in the view. Stretching from one side to the other was the half dismantled weir, a mass of large uneven stones, with a height that varied between four and five meters. The water, divided into waterfalls that resembled locks of hair, though not abundant, crashed into the pools on the rocky platform below, foaming and churning, to form various rivulets that joined further on to form a fast-flowing stream strewn with boulders that drained the lake. The weir, they could see it clearly now, had, in times gone by, served a tiny power station, the tower, which had then been abandoned.

"At the speed we were doing, and with the weight of the boat on top of us, it would have been the equivalent of falling two or three floors, or more. Into the pools! Even our bones would have been smashed beyond recognition. Shall we have some lunch?"–And he laughed.

They returned to the car. The little girl had fallen asleep, stretched out on the rear seat. At last, the sun appeared through the ragged clouds and was hot. It was only half an hour after the incident that his heart began to beat hard: a sort of retrospective fear. Or was it out of impotent rage? It was still early. His nerves hadn't recovered yet.

A Tale of Fish

Don't they say that the good King Henry I of England died, somewhat undramatically, of indigestion as a result of eating lamprey? Nor is it just kings who die of this. Maybe there are one or two fatal incidences of gluttony involving this particular delicacy in the novels of Camilo (and if there aren't, there certainly should be): it's a matter I have great pleasure in leaving to the *gourmets* of literature and lampreys.

A curious sequence of ideas has brought me thus far. First, a recent item of news to the effect that a huge, unknown "fish" had been caught already dead on the Algarve coast. Some eight meters in length, and weighing two tons, it (and I quote) "was probably not a whale, but evinced some signs of belonging to the cachalot family." I can tell you that it certainly wasn't a lamprey, any more than it was the Loch Ness monster. The creature amazed the crowds of watchers and ended up being returned to the sea from which it had come, given that no possible use could be found for it.

This reminded me of a story I read years ago in a Luso-American newspaper, reproduced from the press in Portugal, about a twelve- to fourteen-kilo salmon, which had been caught in the River Minho[1], with a wound on its side that was spongy and had not formed a scar, and that because it couldn't be explained, left the locals mystified. Here, as in the case of the "fish" that didn't seem to be a whale but showed signs of being a cachalot, what seems extraordinary to me is the innocence of those who discovered it, wrote about it, or merely looked on. And the fact that there was no zoologist on hand to clarify the mystery.

In the old days, one would quite often read in the papers that thirty or forty thousand young trout, reared on farms in the countryside, had been thrown into some river in the Minho, to increase the population and improve the stock. And that's what intrigued me: where did these young trout and salmon end up–assuming that they reached the age of being caught and grilled–given that they never got as far as the Ribeira fish market or the Praça da Figueira, nor did they get hawked around the streets in the fishwives' baskets, as did the humble sardine from the coast near Lisbon or the distinguished bream from Sesimbra?... Yes indeed, who was growing fat on the rich fruits of our countrymen's efforts during the fishing season?–It is a well-known fact that the province of Asturias has welcomed a considerable number of tourists for some years now, attracted by the fishing of the sturdy native trout (apparently now threatened in its ancestral way of life by the hydroelectric dams); but, as far as I am aware, there has never been this type of tourism in the Minho.

In the window of a well-known victualer's in the Chiado (well okay, call it a "charcuterie" if you prefer the Gallicism with its whiff of *sauerkraut!*), they would very occasionally put on show a juicy red slice of salmon that caused folk to stop and admire it, gazing in wonder and with watery mouth at this rare delicacy, whose inaccessible price made it worthy of the banqueting tables of kings and corn grinders. What was the reason for the scarcity and shortage of these well-loved creatures of the salmon family?

Well now, it was the article in the humble Luso-American newspaper that clarified things for me many years later. Let me tell you how.

The lamprey–*Petromyzon marinus*–is a horrible eel-like fish, slimy and without scales (which is why it counts among its defenders orthodox Jews and other people who are no less respectful of taboos). It is graced with a single nostril on the top of its head and seven gills on each side, which are round like spy-holes. It doesn't have any jaws, but it possesses a round mouth, endowed with a crown of teeth, a real sucker that allows it to fasten itself to the bodies of its favorite fish, which consist mainly of the aristocracy of river and lake-dwelling fauna. It takes them by surprise, and by deception, it clamps its sucker on them, and once it is firmly attached, with the many teeth arranged like a comb along its tongue, it tears their flesh. Clever, as well as cunning and cruel, it injects a chemical substance into the wound that stops the blood from clotting, and in this way, just like any bloodsucker, it sucks it greedily until it has filled its belly and left its victim weakened or dead from loss of blood. At that point, it lets its victim go, in order to return to the murky depths from where it had launched its treacherous assault. I'm dramatizing it a little, but there you are!

You can see now that the salmon with the ulcer on its flank, must have struggled courageously to shake the parasite off; or perhaps it had let go of its own volition, leaving its victim to go and recover from its loss of blood… until the next attack. That's why I sympathize as much with the trout and the salmon as I hate the lamprey. I've only ever tried it once, and I was disgusted; it was a present from someone who thought he owed me for some forgotten favor.

No doubt it is because of this select and exclusive diet that the flesh of the lamprey, which as far as I am concerned has the texture and after-taste of mud, is held in such high esteem by Epicureans. Can you imagine how many victims are needed to make this monster, which is capable of living for many years and of reaching a meter in length? So all this slaughter and the scarcity of trout and salmon on our dinner tables was not just due to poachers and their use of dynamite; the rivers of the Minho were sacrificing their refined and costly population to the lamprey. Yes, indeed, to the lamprey, the bait with which, in olden times, plaintiffs, claimants, solicitants, and petitioners in general, would seek to reward or ensure a propitious verdict, order, favor, or quite simply the expected or already received judicial sentence: The Honorable-Magistrate's-Lamprey.

After this, tell me who can possibly like lamprey; he deserves the same fate as that of King Henry of England. So now, my dear readers, you know who this Diogo Alves of other watery pastures is[2], this preda-tor of our piscicultural stocks, and what he eats (or sucks). My apologies if I made your mouth water.

The North Americans have, as we say, a somewhat "strange palate": they don't eat lamprey, which is such a delicacy and so esteemed among other nations, especially the Latin ones. I don't know whether this is due to the effect of Roman Law. They don't like rabbit either, although an-other rodent, the dear little squirrel, is a traditional prey for them. In compensation, they gorge themselves on delicious trout and salmon. Among the latter, there are some that are so cheap that they are even sold in tins as cat food. Feeding the cat with salmon! Seen from the Chiado, this seems like heresy. Or from the Minho, for that matter.

Be that as it may, when an invasion of lampreys threatened to wipe out from their rivers and lakes the trout population, a source of wealth and the focus of numerous amateur sportsmen, the Americans sought to block its access by placing nets across the beds of watercourses. I don't know how successful this has been. I've never seen a lamprey on sale. But the lamprey, a representative of the oldest, most primitive form of vertebrate, has its mouth-like sucker to thank for being able to climb up steps, weirs and dams, against waterfalls and cataracts, in order to go and spawn–just like the trout and the salmon–in its own distant places. It's one of these instances of a prodigious ability to survive that leaves us gaping with astonishment, as if we were looking at a salmon in the Chiado, and it makes one realize that Nature protects both the *gangster* and his victim–what a mysterious dialectic! It's true that it has its own enemies and parasites, such as the sinister hagfish, and that its eggs and larvae are eaten by other fish, which helps to re-establish equilibrium (or should I say justice?) in natural life.

As for us Portuguese, given that there aren't enough lampreys to satisfy all candidates and solicitants, or the appetite of the providers of dispatches and sinecures, we have invented the egg lamprey, a truly admirable substitute! And this one I certainly do like. But please don't send me one through the mail or by courier; the most likely outcome will be that although it is made of eggs, Uncle Sam's customs barriers won't let it through.

Notes

[1] The northernmost province in Portugal, and also the name of the river that forms the northern border with the Spanish region of Galicia. (Translator's note.)

[2] Diogo Alves was a famous murderer in nineteenth-century Lisbon, who lured his victims onto the city's aqueduct, robbed them and threw them over the edge. He was caught and hanged in 1841. (Translator's note.)

An Indian Polychrome

In his *Writer's Notebook*, Somerset Maugham has left us some brief but candid impressions of a visit he made to Goa in 1938. Such as the Portuguese church where the native choir sang, accompanied by the organ; the somewhat harsh voices gave the Catholic hymns "a mysteriously pagan, Indian character". A priest in his early thirties went to visit him in his hotel. He was tall and of good appearance and told him in excellent English that he was from a Brahmanic family and that one of his forebears had been converted to Christianity by a companion of Saint Francis Xavier. A preacher, he spent a lot of time converting the Sudras; but with the high-class Hindus, the task of conversion was a hopeless one. "Even among the Christians–he said–the system of castes still persisted, to the extent that none of them would marry outside their own caste. It would be unheard of for a Christian from a Brahman family to marry a woman of Sudra origin. It wasn't without some pleasure that he declared that he did not have one drop of Christian blood in his veins; the family had always remained resolutely pure.–We are Christians–he said–but above all we are Hindus."

And Maugham continues: "He thought Christianity was broad enough to encapsulate all other beliefs, but he bemoaned the fact that Rome had not allowed the Indian church to develop in harmony with local cultural identification. I was left with the impression that he accepted the dogmas of the Church as a discipline, but without any fervor;

I sense that although he had four hundred years of Catholicism behind him, at heart he was still a Vedantist, and I wondered whether, for him, the God of the Christians had not been absorbed into the Brahma of the Upanishads…"

This reminded me of an episode from my teenage years. One day, in Lisbon, my father introduced me to a venerable Indian clergyman of his acquaintance. A gray-haired man, of indefinable age, as is often the case with people from the tropics, modestly dressed and wearing scruffy boots, Monsignor X had an aristocratic Portuguese surname that I don't recall. He was rather slow on his feet. Some time afterwards, I met him in the Almirante Reis. He invited me up to his flat, a very modest third or fourth-floor dwelling in the Brás Simões quarter (later christened the English quarter): the hovel of a poorly paid Indian servant of Christ. In the almost bare living room, with its few paltry sticks of furniture, he showed me a truly beautiful collection of English prints, colored like images of d'Epinal, representing scenes from the bloody Sepoy Rebellion of 1857-58. In the last scene, the intrepid Nana-Sahib, who had been one of the leaders of the insurrection, dignified in defeat, surrounded by a glowing array of military commanders from both camps, and dressed with all the pomp of a raja, held out his saber in surrender to the victorious British commander. He, the picture of probity, held out his hands in a respectful gesture of refusal. (Can it be that I am mistaken about this episode? Nana-Sahib, defeated repeatedly by Generals Havelick and Campbell, took refuge in Nepal, where he eventually died. But the important thing here is the significance of the act.)

My clergyman friend, doubly Portuguese in name and in religion, commented: "See how the English treat their vanquished like gentlemen, with all the honors due to a noble, loyal adversary, a patriot! What did we do to Gungunhana, the leader of the Vatuas? We put him, laden with chains, in the hold of a ship, and went and paraded him before the Court in London[1] as if he were a monkey, with a collar round his neck, and then we let him die ingloriously in a dungeon in Angra do Heroismo!"

I honestly cannot recall how the conversation finished… or was it a lesson? I left the place confused and convinced that the Monsignor was not a patriot, nor a Portuguese, or else he had never read a single page of history that might be classified as "sincere". Was he unaware of the great violence and cruelty the British had exercised in India? I didn't see him again, but the episode left me with a strong gut feeling that none of the texts, lectures, lessons and preaching of the experts and ideologues, great and small, good and bad, for and against, that I read or heard after that, managed to erase. Could he be a relative of Somerset Maugham's Goan priest? I ask myself now.

In the 1920s, I used to frequent downtown Lisbon, where I got to know and became friends with an Indian, a Catholic with a Portuguese name, who told me he belonged to the noble caste of the Shatrias, or warrior-princes, which, according to his somewhat simplistic version of Indian history, had been dethroned and subjugated by the Brahmans. I never got to understand, nor did he explain it to me, how it was that these brave warriors allowed themselves to be subverted by the unarmed priests. He harbored a sort of ancestral resentment against the usurpers, and it was maybe this factor that led him to style himself a "communist". I laughed… He pressed me to introduce him to Jaime Cortesão, at the time Director of the National Library. Authorized by the latter, I took him to São Francisco, where, for half-an-hour, he massacred the historian with a nervous and loquacious exposition of the hardships suffered by his noble caste. This, I imagine, was pure propaganda. Once he'd had his say, he left. After formally seeing him to the door of his office, Cortesão turned to me and said: "Your Shatria friend left me shattered!"

Some time later, Gonzaga (let's call him that) accosted me excitedly in Rossio Square: "We're no longer friends!" he said. "You betrayed our friendship. You showed me no consideration!" Mystified, I laughed and asked him why. He replied: "Last night, you spent hours walking up and down here with Eucaristino de Mendonça!" "What nonsense! Isn't he a Catholic, Portuguese Indian like yourself? And a poet to boot!"

Eucarastino de Mendonça was a thin lad, pleasant and somewhat sad, no doubt poor, dark-skinned but with delicate features, a perfect example–as far as I could see–of the race of "princes", a pure Arian, in contrast to Gonzaga, who had lighter coloring, but rather gross, Dravidian features. In 1924, he had published and given me a copy of his slim book of poems–*Hindus, poemas indianos*–composed with all the pseudo-oriental embellishments that were then in fashion among us, and full of artless flourishes, Indian phonemes, italics, mistakes in metrification and spelling. I think the author died not long afterwards of tuberculosis. Maybe from a surfeit of poetic *bijouterie*?

Gonzaga bellowed angrily: "He's a *Sudra*! And I'm a Shatria! We've got nothing in common!" My comment must have been short and to the point: "You're out of your mind!"

Our relationship cooled somewhat. A few years went by, and I read in a paper that he had joined the government party. As an unemployed

English teacher, he was trying to get onto the staff of a state secondary school. The gesture neither surprised nor made any impression on me; it was his affair. One morning, I was sitting on my own in the almost deserted *Brasileira* on Rossio Square, when he came in and approached me. I did not invite him to sit down at my table. Standing there, he began to explain why he had joined the party. Thinking this unnecessary, I politely asked him not to continue. Agitated, he denied that he was giving me justifications. In that case, what were they? I asked him. He returned to the fray–he needed to earn some bread and so on–by which time I was getting irritated (I couldn't stand seeing a man making a fool of himself) and shouted out loud: "They are justifications! I don't want to listen to them! Keep them to yourself!" My voice, as if surprised at its own strength, reverberated off the mirrors and the few customers turned to look at us. As he wouldn't stop talking, I bellowed: "Go away! Don't bother me and don't speak to me again!" Then, ashen-faced, he took a step back and said: "Very well, then. Good day!" And he went and sat down somewhere else. I turned in my chair, and looked at him.

Sitting in a row against the mirrors were four or five Indians, silent, motionless, devoid of expression. I was unable to read any thought or feeling–anger, irony, whatever–in those gleaming dark eyes, those smooth, round, dark faces, without so much as a wrinkle; they were impenetrable. Wow! I confess that such impassiveness made me feel small. And there was Gonzaga. The café fell back into its sleepy morning silence, and I finished drinking my dose.

I realized then that these men were not my spiritual brethren, they were not Portuguese (like the clergyman). It was the first time that I was able to measure the void, or the abyss, that separated us: four hundred years of racial and cultural intimacy, of bureaucracy and proselytizing, of baptisms and noble family names, had not created any unity of character among us. (This, in spite of the numerous cases of fertile loyalty showed by so many Indo-Portuguese, some of them illustrious ones.)

In the friendly contact maintained by Indo-Portuguese intellectuals, attracted to the *Seara Nova* group by António Sérgio, who was himself the son of an Indian mother, I had already come to realize that their philosophical attitude had nothing in common with either our idealistic, metaphysical, reformist rationalism, or with the various nuances of Western materialism; it was more an eclectic mysticism, fashioned out of more or less amalgamated and badly assimilated Hindu traditions, which featured the Vedas, Karma, Metempsychosis, Rabindranath Tagore, Gandhi, Annie Besant, Krishna Murti... everything which, ever since

Schopenhauer, as far as I can see, and the Aryanism of Max Muller and others, has become fashionable in the West, and above all in the Anglo-American world: the Orientalism, or Indianism, that has fascinated many good folk, including Romain Rolland and Hermann Hesse.

Wherever they could, possibly as disappointed Catholics, they spread their belief, as vague as it was legitimate, in Indian "ideals"–if indeed it could be said that these corresponded to any body of unified doctrines–and in a certain pacifism and asceticism that stood in brazen contradiction to so many Indian legends, the fabulously erotic architecture of so many ancient temples in Hindustan and the implacable inhumanity of the religious, linguistic, racial, political and other violence for which India has been a theater.

I myself had even enrolled in a course of Sanskrit given by the Indian expert, Monsignor Dalgado, only to give up after two or three lessons, terrified by what I saw as the insuperable difficulties of the alphabet. But neither a reading of Romain Rolland and G. Le Bon, nor (much later) E.M. Forster's *A Passage to India*, not to mention sociologists, theosophists and spiritualists of all types, would wrest me from my ignorance of what India was really like. I am not embarrassed to confess that it is only now, having read Ved Mehta's *Portrait of India* (the record of an extensive and long-lasting journey), that I have acquired a clear general appreciation of that vast and mysterious sub-continent where, over a period of a few millennia, there has been an unsystematic juxtaposition (or better, superimposition) of races, languages, beliefs, cultures and philosophies, castes, customs and prejudices, the splendor of great wealth and the most atrocious poverty, beauty and horror, hatred and incompatibility–to turn India into what is for us an insoluble puzzle, something that far exceeds all that our Western imagination could conceive.

It is no small miracle that a country of such historical, geographical and human diversity, with more than 450 million inhabitants, speaking more than eight hundred languages and major dialects, and where there are a dozen religions and countless mutually hostile sects, manages to maintain a relative or precarious political unity, when Europe, which is far more homogeneous and no less proud of its civilization, has been split for two thousand years by ignorance and war.

If India has much to learn from the West, isn't the opposite also true?

Note

[1] Gungunhana, or Ngungunhane (1850?-1906), was a nguni ruler who resisted Portuguese incursions into Southern Mozambique until his capture in 1895. He was in fact taken to Lisbon (not London), where he was paraded in the streets before being exiled in the Azores, where he died. (Translator's note.)

Bowery '64

On the other side of the street, which was very wide at this point, a man lies flat, his head resting on the edge of the sidewalk, and his eyes wide open. He's young and seems calm. Not far away, a policeman, perhaps an Italian, waves his arms around and laughs. Further on, in a side street, the ambulance waits: for whom? For what? It's eleven o'clock on a Saturday morning; there is a weak sun and not much traffic. Scattered around some distance away, other men stand watching the scene silently. I've stopped to look too. From time to time, the injured man raises his head, lifts his hand to his curly blond hair, which is soaked in blood, examines it carefully, maybe with pride, and once again places it cautiously on his chest. Blood stains his face and shirt and flows into the gutter. (If I ask the cause, no one answers.)

At this point, on the edge of the sidewalk on my side of the street, two black women in little hats and sheets of paper in their hands, one of them young, the other graying, and both of them skinny, launch tunelessly and with rasping voices into a hymn, which reinforces the puritanical numbness of the air. One of them is holding a little star spangled flag–just in case they're taken for communists! Occasionally a bus or truck passes by and drowns out their voices that are more reminiscent of Purgatory than of Heaven. No one seems to hear them. Who are they singing for? When they raise their eyes from their hymn sheets, it is not to look at men, but the dull sun or the fronts of buildings, from where no head peeps out. Some evangelical organization employs them to visit the Bowery and remind men who have fallen that there is a Heaven, an Eternity and a reward for virtue. Seeds–or ashes?–thrown into the wind! All those men know is that Hell exists and it has already arrived. *Jesus is life!* They gain it humbly, while the others lose it, drowned in sin and whiskey.

Eça, who passed through here a hundred years ago ("Loathsome New York–no, adorable New York!"), wouldn't recognize it. Luxury carriages rolled along the streets in those days, there were expensive restaurants, and an opera house. (The Amato Opera still exists, but only at a local level; and the Bowery Follies, for discerning monster lovers, employs decadent old artists from the Varieties or the Vaudeville and the Burlesque; they are capable of making even the cement between the paving stones weep!) The only things left from the olden days are the façades of the buildings, the false grandeur of which, over time, and contrary to custom, has become truly hair-raising. But there is a character about them... Nor is it the same Bowery I knew, in the days of Roosevelt and the New Deal. In 1937, with some seven million unemployed, there were still hundreds and thousands of pariahs who came here to hide their failures or their timidity, sell the rags on their body (the open-air market still exists), drink, start quarrels, punch each other, sleep in the entrances or on the steps of buildings or along the sidewalks. Not all of them had the money to pay for a bed in one of the many overnight hotels in the area, some with pompous names such as "Palace" or "Florida"; and if they did have it, they preferred to spend it on drink: alcohol softens the hardest stone pillow; and even among the destitute there are class distinctions. At night, and in the middle of the day, which was always gloomy here, one would stumble over bodies lying flat out, curled up, lifeless. The complex shadow of the "El" was benevolent to those whom fortune had disinherited. From the elevated train, one could see, as it passed by, into the lounges of these hotels, where the unemployed, the tramps, the homeless, the vanquished (the word sounds obsolete to me!) huddled together, solitary beings among their crowd, wearing berets or hats, sleeping, playing cards, reading a paper, or quite simply not doing anything: waiting in desperation. The dim, copper colored sun cast a burnt glow on men and things. The Bowery offered the shameless face of the Crisis to reporters from all over the world, anxious to see the mote in the eye of their fellow man, and to ignore the plank in their own.

Crime never took root in this part of town; gangsters don't want anything to do with these humiliated, impotent people, who have chosen a life of resignation, and the police hardly ever come here. On the other hand, and this defies explanation, one occasionally sees two or three policemen making a show of beating a *bum* or a drunk: could this possibly be in order to revive in them the physical notion of the State and Authority? As the Second World War got closer, the crisis lessened, and the Bowery lost many of its guests. The structure of the "El" was demolished–thousands of tons of steel bought by the Japanese for a song, in order to build the fleet with which they would face the United States in the Pacific. (Scrap loses only ten percent of its original steel when recast.) Roads were resurfaced, the place was cleaned up, buildings were knocked down, and façades were renovated, and the *bums* retreated like rats chased out by the newly revealed light. Poverty is furtive. Many of the hotels closed down, but not all; and there are still some dark, gloomy bars and restaurants that exploit these outcasts. The Salvation Army has built a new hostel–music on an electric organ, bible readings over a loudspeaker, coffee and bread–and the reprobates look on from afar, timidly and greedily, at the Lord's bait. Near here, on Third Street, there is a Welfare dormitory and canteen, which nowadays caters mainly for Blacks and assimilated Puerto Ricans; Harlem has overflowed into all areas of the city, and equality is being created on the lowest rungs of society by former rivals. Throughout the area, in the doorways, in the ruins, the piles of rubble and the waste ground, among the piles of trash and waste metal (everything here is rust colored), there are piles of bottles and empty cans.

Who are, who were these unfortunate souls, so many of them bruised, blood-stained, their eyes drained of color underneath the arnica, dressed in rags or ill-fitting borrowed clothes, who spill onto the neighboring streets and avenues, smelling of many a heavy punch and begging? Many of them are proud and don't beg; others stare at us with an amused or tearful, but supplicating look in their eye. There are those who like to engage one in conversation, with the social niceties of alcoholics anxious to give the impression of being sober and smart; and there are those who were something in life and in business, and were toppled from the social heights of Madison or Park Avenue, and came in search of obscurity and to be forgotten: for competition among the vanquished produces less anxiety than it does among the triumphant. And whiskey always tastes the same.

One morning in 1964, I paused to look in the dusty window of a second-hand bookshop belonging to "Book Mart", near Fourth Avenue. From a nearby doorway, a gentle voice called me: *"Are you hungry?"* For a moment I was taken aback–could it be that I looked as if…?–and then I was moved: how many years is it since I was asked that question! "No, and you?" "Yes, I am!" It was an old man (maybe younger than me), decent and modest, with the gentlest look in his clear, transparent eyes. I never refuse money to these poor souls, not even when they are drunk and insist that it's for a coffee or a bowl of soup: "What the hell! Aren't the Others up there getting drunk at this hour?" A black man answered, trying to embrace me: *"Sir, you are a true gentleman!"* They don't get any richer, nor I any poorer. And I can't (nor do I want to) save them! On another occasion, on First Avenue, as I was on my way to do some shopping in the open-air market, I was accosted by a tall, upstanding old man, with blue eyes, long, refined features, a brusque manner and the rolling walk of a former seaman: "I'm hungry!"–holding out his hand. What must such men feel, after a life spent on the sea that sapped them of their blood and their dreams, when they find themselves on dry land without a crust, and have to demean themselves by begging? Lord, how this pains me! I gave him 25 cents. He looked at the silver coin in the palm of his long hand– *"Jesus Christ, a quarter!"*–and he walked off with a flourish, without saying thank you. No doubt he thought: "A quarter of a dollar, things have come to this! Money either isn't worth anything or it insults us. And here am I hungry!"

But what dignity, and sometimes even what beauty and drama there are among these wretched people! Supreme individualists (although there are fewer of them now with the increasing numbers of Blacks and Latin Americans), used to facing storms on the high seas and life's perils–every man for himself and God for all–they feel alienated in the world of the unions, the collective contract, the minimum wage, working hours, double time, social security in old age, during unemployment and in sickness or disability, all these the guarantees and privileges that other men, with audacity and a spirit of self-sacrifice, often paying with their freedom and their life, have managed to gain for the exploited and oppressed. This "collectivism" goes against their grain, invades their *privacy* and restricts their personal independence, their Anglo-Saxon stamp. They don't want to feel Society's dependants, not even if it mothers them. They are *Men!* And as such, enemies of the powers that be and of bureaucracy. They prefer to consider themselves, to call themselves "free", and to live and die as such, than to depend on the State, on Assistance or on a Union that, to their thinking, exploits them and steals away their spirit of initiative. Rather, then, this world of risks and contrasts, brotherhood and whiskey, that Dickens, Dostoievsky, Hal Caine, Sean O'Casey, G.B. Shaw, O'Neill, Brecht and Orwell, among others, depicted with different styles and tones, sometimes embittered and pessimistically, sometimes evangelical and hopefully: in the name of Christ, of Socialism, or of nothing at all.

But why am I talking about these people, you may ask? What is it that attracts me to these marginals? (There's always some hidden reason for what we write about!) Can it be some desire to identify myself with those who are anonymous, voiceless, dependent? Is it my intuitive fate? The genetic echo of some "Bocanegra"[1] (what a name for a *condottiere!*) that flows in my blood? Or is it merely an inclination to show charity? I don't lament, on the contrary I applaud, the changes in the world and its fortunes; nor do I censure these people–indeed, I sympathize with them. Many are victims out of choice, in so far as this is possible in this world of ours: *free!* Prosperity, like freedom, has its flip side, its thorns, and not all men go as far as falling quite so low. Our repudiation of poverty is almost always born out of our fear of it, the subjectivization of other people's suffering; or the suppression of our attraction for irresponsibility ("deep down all of us have something of the anarchist in us!"), or who knows, self-destruction. On the other hand, love of the wretched is perhaps the opposite of real love: because it tries to preserve them in the aspic of their indigence. In order to eliminate poverty it is not enough to join it, as Orwell did in his poignant book of personal experiences, *Down and Out in London and Paris*. Something more is needed–a faith, an idea, a technique, a will. Only these will put an end to the Boweries of this world, along with their fascinating and inhuman picturesque atmosphere.

I walk slowly down the street and, listening to the Black female evangelists, I fancy I see dark-skinned cherubs flying over this hell.

Why didn't I bring a cameraman with me to film these contrasts?

Note

[1] The Bocanegras were descended from a well-known Genoese political family (the Boccaneras). In Italy, Simón Boccanera sided with the 'people' in uprisings against the aristocracy during the fourteenth century, while in Spain, he fought in the Reconquest. Francisco Bocanegra came to Portugal in the retinue of the Spanish wife of King John III. He married a Portuguese noble-woman, but was suspected of being a crypto-Jew. Miguéis is playing with the reputation of the Bocanegras as being a vaguely populist, transnational family. (Ttranslator's note.)

The Happy Christmas Story I Didn't Write

Who knows? Maybe "inspiration" will fall from the heavens or from the cornices, or rise from the pavement; it wouldn't be the first time. A happy story is full of warmth and has what poor things here call a "happy end", isn't that what they are asking for? I've written them in the past, in total opposition to my experience and my ideological stance, in which it all ends badly. These festive days always… but lets not get bitter! Maybe this girl who is traveling next to me on the Sixth Avenue "local": the air of an anemic English woman of uncertain age, prominent forehead, blue-gray eyes, long chin, dull, straight unkempt hair falling over her shoulders, slender neck, in all a figure that I find intriguing. There are problems, a morbid touch about her… a Hippy! With so many packets and crumpled carrier bags, is she taking presents to her family? Or is she moving? Between two stations, we look at each other with a vague smile of understanding. Only now do I notice the man who accompanies her not far away, in the seat which is perpendicular to hers. Isn't that strange? Younger than me, but downcast, his dank hair in strands, his clear eyes painfully tired, his mustache drooping. She looks at him meaningfully, and then stares at me again, her humid, tearful smile, as if telling me what? That they are married, perhaps? Or long-term partners, always a case of that with me, what luck? Is that it? Heck… I glance at myself in the grubby glass out of the corner of my eye—I don't look my age, ten-fifteen years younger, and I'm not sad either, I who have reason to be so and look it! (Or is it just pretense on my part?) This vivaciousness… And I'm still hot-blooded. Suddenly, she leans towards me and says something that I don't understand at first because of the noise of the wheels (nor a second time), but in the end I hear her words: "Hasn't anyone told you that you look just like William Faulkner?" I almost fall off my seat. Never! I reply carelessly: "But that's all we have in common, the biggest difference being that I'm still alive!…" Now, if it wasn't for that man there, I might even consider following her to one of those apartments in the Village, where apparent freedoms lie hidden and failures are fatalistically accepted–a living-room, bathroom and kitchen, or "kitchenette", a divan that serves as a bed and a sofa, with hard springs and faded cushions, a weak light and dust-filled sadness… But there's not a spark of interest now. It's a holiday, and these folk… He smiles, unaware. I look out of the window:

Forty-Second Street! And I wanted to get out at Fourth Street! I leap up and step onto the platform. Look where I've ended up. Ever this obsession–a fantasy, refuge or escape, age, that's all we've got left… There's always a commitment, a job, an urgent matter, a distance that separates me from these hypothetical objectives. If I pass a girl or a woman in the street who pleases me or who looks at me in a friendly way, says "hello" to me in a low voice or asks for some unnecessary information, we are always walking in opposite directions, and I never have the courage to turn on my heel and follow her. (I don't know whether you have noticed that people who are walking in the same direction hardly ever meet.) If it's on the Subway, or a streetcar, and if she gets off before I do (and I don't follow her), or if I'm the one who gets off first because I'm on my way somewhere, what a pity, and I feel her look of irony or censure on my back. How many times have I lost an opportunity, or think I have lost one, in such circumstances! But it's better to lose than to be disappointed. They pass by and I stay where I am. Or I'm the one who passes by and everything stays as it is. "Au revoir, until never again!" And I ponder once more over that poem–Where we're going is where we are and where we are is what's important…(That's me and Poetry!)

I wandered for some time through Times Square and Forty-Second Street, past all the pornography and celluloid, and suddenly I'm on Fifth Avenue. One can't break through the throng. This voracious festive crowd getting ready for the holiday! Incandescent window displays, cascades of lights, artificial plants, festooned shop-fronts that inundate us with the heavenly music of their electric organs or tape-recorders, and display glamorized nativity scenes of first-class comfort, with moving magi, angels with clarions or flutes or mandolins in the late medieval style, gleaming, borax snow and gold and silver icicles… There is laughter and there are cries of joy and astonishment, truncated exclamations, flushed faces, kisses, and my sense of humor is beginning to addle. (Stay calm and collected, you've got a story to write!) The towers of Rockefeller Center are floodlit and look as if they are made of glass. The air pulsates and is suffused with light, aromas, and a mixture of sounds. The grass is so green that it looks artificial and is dotted with mannequins (or are they angels) of exquisite taste, straight out of some medieval pageant–or Froissart's chronicles, the luxury edition, gilt-edged, with enamel inlay and special metal clips. I can't resist admiring and envying them. What skill these fellows have! Down below, in the ice-rink, people skate to the sound of a Viennese waltz, and above the packed crowds, angelic voices hover, singing Noël, Noël, or "Silent night, Holy night…" But what's this? A Christmas Circus? Lord Jesus, get me out of here fast! (At this rate, I won't get anywhere, and instead of a story, it'll be a pamphlet.) A group of French sailors and young officers, their faces fresh and ruddy, Bretons from a novel by Loti or Farrère, and abandoned here, laugh, talk, take photos, film… L'Amérique!

On top of a steel platform that has been erected somewhat arbitrarily and at a great height, as if in a circus, a cameraman–in leather jacket and fur collar, hat and gloves–focuses his huge television camera (NBC-TV), pointing it at the decorations and the folk who wave and gesticulate, thrilled: Me too! Me too! Then, he draws himself up straight, tall and youthful, a space "cowboy" or lunar "superman", dominating the scene from on high, phlegmatic and proud, shy and nervous no doubt: the perfect figure for the cover of a science fiction novel. I feel my irrepressible hostility to the mechanics of putting on a "show", to gadgets, the mass media, to the general imbecility of these and other lesser shenanigans. What have Christ and Stravinsky to do with this? But isn't it the case that I'm being dragged into it?… (Well, okay, lets not allow ourselves to be affected by considerations that… Lets keep our mind on the story!) And I return to Fifth Avenue.

The man is standing, his back to the wall, watching the streams of onlookers. He is middle-aged, decently dressed, dark and stern, he could be Greek, Sicilian or Portuguese. (But not Spanish: the severity of the Spaniard is always aggressive and disdainful, and this man knows how to mingle and impose himself.) I feel less alone, as if I could discern in his air of an outsider at a party in full swing the Other Me, searching for a lost or imaginary world that no longer exists in space or time. (We always return to the Future!) As he looks around reproachfully, his gaze tells me that he is sad, that he doesn't approve of the "show", the commercialization of Christmas, and the surroundings that alienate him. That's what he thinks and I think. What is he looking for then, what is he waiting for? To become less alienated, to participate and belong, to mingle, or to preserve his difference, to remain absent and strong? To be himself and suffer the consequences, or to be someone else, to become indistinguishable from the rest and abandon his own beliefs!... For it is this, I can see in his face, that is making him suffer. And yet it is this rancor and suffering that preserves our identity! (Deep down, it is envy.) Fiddlesticks! I'm just trying to invent, discover, stumble across a Christmas story! But from the frozen heavens, blood-red from the illuminations, nothing comes to me. Not even snow. And I don't drink, sir, that's another vice of mine! (My mind has begun to wander, I'm ready.) I feel confused. It's because I don't know whether I detest them or envy them. Everything that seemed to me to be clear and distinct, moral and rational categories—good and evil, beauty and ugliness, hatred and love, idealism and reality, space and time, necessity and contingency, thesis and antithesis, cause and effect, chance and mischance, sameness and difference, rebellion and submission, the world, men, events, ideas, facts, doctrines—everything seems to have lost its contours, to have become obscure, indecipherable, fused into this shapeless process of continuity, gray, homogenous and plural, a Chaos from which the Spirit is absent (or has not yet emerged), and through which I drift, or hurl myself, like some unicellular being or some loose particle. I am no longer capable of defining, choosing between one thing and another, resisting, reaching a decision. I am paralyzed. But writing is to some extent like taking an action in that it requires choice and commitment: to a particular way of doing things, to an attitude, style, emotion, system, condition or group. To imagine, invent, create is to define, to limit or restrain oneself, to contest and take up a position. And, as a protagonist, I feel myself both at one with it all and removed. My stories, subjects, settings, characters become ambiguous, diffuse, imprecise, personal and yet impersonal. Maybe I am prone to too much analysis, as people have already told me. If I can't adopt a stance and choose, no matter how objective or how much of an observer I may believe myself to be, it is impossible for me to write, to create characters, to awaken emotions: to carve out of this Chaos—me and the world, my world—a shape, a body, a story or a clear route... And I promised you a Christmas story, and a happy one too, if possible! This sudden and alarming feeling of impotence paralyzes me to the extent of even preventing me from making an effort. The only consciousness I have, and even this is vague, is that I am and I exist, that is I am fixed but I am becoming, I am stability and movement, unity and plurality. I, who saw everything clearly, or thought I did, suffer yet again. From what? Why? And what is suffering? Is it the last refuge for our individual capacity for self-affirmation and reaction? The last convulsion of an idealism in its death throes, of our understanding of the individual's (frustrated) role in his world? (Nothing exists there, everything's over here… says the poem!) Am I just an inert part of all this, or a distinct entity, an observer, an agent? And if so, am I aggressive?… Rancor, revolt, satire, even when they are objectively justified and necessary, are a last-ditch attempt to conceal from our own eyes the bitterness at having lost or never having reached, possessed or taken control of that which we dreamt of aspiring to, and this causes us a deep, dark pain; or else it is to mask our rejection, whether sincere or feigned, of this very condition… I no longer know what to believe in, nor how to believe! I'm like the lover who might say: "I reject your love in favor of the love of the other woman, whose love I rejected out of love for you…" And can it be that they understand all this? Understand what a tragic illusion, a trap, this is? And to think that this is how I feel just before Christmas! (The man is still standing on the corner. To hell with him!) I never feel so insignificant, so much a stranger (I've always been like this), so ephemeral and weak, so poor and deprived of everything, I who am happy with so little, as when I find myself among these festive and easily satisfied multitudes. Could it be that my desires were too great, and that's why I deprive myself and give up? All I have are questions, for I've run out of answers! Not even the sun in all its entirety, nor the air, nor all the love, hatred and glory in the world could satisfy me now: is that it? And yet I do not fight to attain anything. I'm still the poor kid who looked in at shop windows and other children's Christmas toys; the permanent exile or refugee, "alive among the living, but invisible and alone" wherever he goes, whose desire is to be with the living and the dead, the present and the absent, the accommodating and the unaccommodating, friends and enemies, past and future, the near and the far, reality and illusion, united with everything and everyone in space and time. And as this is impossible, he turns his back on it all and remains alone. In the end, what I feel is neither envy nor hatred: it's self-censorship and self-pity. (Once upon a time, all this kingdom was mine, / as far as the eye could see…)

The "Superman" once again peers through the monster's visor, looks at his wristwatch, and adjusts his machine. The "show" is about to begin. Come in, gentlemen, come on in! The fair of all the vanities in the world is going to begin, the Christmas Circus! The light in this open-air film set is blinding. The crowd throngs together, gasps with surprise, gets excited, twists and turns, and laughs, wrapped in fur mufflers, in make-up, in light and glitter. It occurs to me that some are at war: in the jungle, the mud, the blood, in their nakedness, hunger, darkness and pain, in hell. What are these folk looking for, then? To stifle the guilty conscience of this latter-day empire, that was never intended, and that drags them towards the abyss? The dead, above all the useless dead, the maimed and those beyond salvation, those who are without faults but pay for the faults of others, or die from the illusion they nourished, writing on the wall of their cell the name of the idol who betrayed them (who betrayed us all), or who set themselves alight in some auto-da-fé designed to express the love of life? Noël, Noël! Silent night, Holy night…Dingalingdong! Adeste fideles…! But how can they believe in life, in Christ, in the resurrection, if at each stage they deny it all and sell their soul? In what manger–what Egypt–what jungle is He hiding? And I realize that I am defining myself, that I am beginning once again to see and believe, I make my point, I become consistent–and suddenly I know I don't envy them… And I look for the man from a little while ago, maybe to invite him for a "drink". We'll chat, and talk of our bitterness and scorn, our unhappiness and disappointment. Who knows whether I might not even manage to… explain things, convince him… I look around: he's vanished! He's committed suicide by submersion. He has ceased to exist, unless it was all an illusion of mine, a hallucination. Did I perhaps invent him? Or could he be my double? Or the devil, or who knows, Christ in disguise, contemplating the sad fruit of his Calvary?

Once again, I find myself alone among the electronic-angelic voices, in the midst of the living, I who dreamt of resuscitating the dead (or resuscitating myself from among them.) To be born again at each instant, or from time to time: isn't that the message of the Holy Solstice? That's why we celebrate it. Life that is perpetually reborn out of our ashes, the Christ from among the dead, the eternal becoming, the hope or certainty of the day as night submerges us. But not today, it's late. It's late now. How many years have I had to put up with this! Everything beginning again, on another level and maybe in another life, in another world. I pass by and they remain. (Like the women!) Let them be. My Christmas is something else, my Cross another. I am always going in the opposite direction, against the crowd.

I walk down Fifth Avenue, the crowds thin out, the light and the noise grow dim, just like the decorations. Until I penetrate the dark, silent, deserted quarter once more.

I didn't, after all, have an idea! Oh well, too bad, maybe next year. I shan't be writing the Happy Christmas Story today.

A Dead Hack

The man is tall and portly, middle-aged, looks as if he might be a traveling salesman, with his briefcase brimming with invoice slips and orders, and is lying flat out on the asphalt, almost next to the sidewalk, in the greasy shadow of a parked truck. His eyes are open, unmoving and glassy, his tongue is showing, his chin drawn back and his jowl hanging loose, his puffy face is pink. He's clearly the victim of a heart attack. (I've seen them die like this before in the corridors of the Subway.) He is surrounded by the inquisitive, all of them Puerto Ricans—only they would have the audacity, in this country, to approach a man who had fallen to the ground! They have loosened his collar, undone his tie, and one of them, crouching, cradles his inert head. Another holds his pulses and makes him go through the rhythmic movements of artificial respiration (just in time!). A third impassively rubs his chest lightly in circular movements, there where he imagines his heart to be. While they attempt to revive him, they talk and explain the situation to the bystanders in the pompous, philosophically scientific language inherited from their Iberian forefathers.

It is six o'clock in the evening and the crowd of people making their way home is growing. Someone has phoned the police, and an ambulance should be along soon. Touched by what is happening, I walk away. (I've been living here for two days, and this is what I have to witness so soon...) Then I see rushing toward me with solicitous, careful steps, the owner of the wine and liquor store on the corner, with a glass of whiskey in his hand—*I mustn't spill it! Will I get there in time to save him?* I stop and turn to watch this moving collective attempt to offer the stricken man first-aid. The group of onlookers has swollen, and they all talk and offer their opinions. I can hear the ambulance siren…

The man from the liquor store returns with fleeting little steps but dragging his soles, still holding his brimming glass. He stops next to me and I hear him say: "But he's dead! What good would it do him?" He pauses and looks at his glass of *rye*, the color of burnished gold (*I can't waste this*), then he raises it carefully to his lips, and swallows it in one go.

The womenfolk have just lit some candles for the dead man, and some are kneeling round him.

A Night of Panic Failure

No one can say for sure how this started: maybe it has always been like this; much less can anyone say when it will end: never, in all probability. Nothing begins or ends. This was possibly the first visible symptom of a continuous process that we call "sudden change", like those that we perceive with the passing of time, when they have become telescoped in the past, or when they are so far advanced that we can no longer stop or remedy them and always without measuring their extension, importance or severity. The world undergoes transformations, and we can only see the details, never the grand picture.

It was at the peak hour–it was Autumn and night had already fallen–when after one or two timid but worrying warnings, the power suddenly failed, plunging the city into darkness, and with it, some forty million human beings in the metropolitan area. The underground, overground and surface trains came to a halt; factories, offices, cinemas and cabarets, bars, restaurants and cafés, tens of radio and television stations, all stopped working; in hospitals, brain and stomach operations of the most serious kind were suspended, putting patients at serious risk.

Here and there, in the city that has ground to a standstill, like a film *still*, one or two lights shine, all the more brightly it seems, in institutions miraculously endowed with their own sources of energy. Innumerable crowds, at a deathly slow rate, silently and in fear–but fortunately not overcome by panic–flock down the endless streets and avenues, between high, glass-fronted buildings. People mutter the word "sabotage". But by whom? There haven't been any serious labor conflicts lately, everyone seems to be well-provided, content: the peace of wartime reigns among all social classes. Naturally, people think of the Potential Enemy, and look apprehensively at the sky, which is exceptionally clear, and where, unusually (or perhaps we have never noticed it before), a full and seemingly monstrous moon rises and glides softly: As if we were waiting for squadrons of enemies to suddenly appear, my-God-let-it-not-be-yet, coming to pulverize us with their multimegaton inventions. (We are in the age of the Mega, Oh Mega!) But the enemy wouldn't attack like that, to begin with it would be invisible, silent… Exactly! Listen then: no one can hear the rumble of an engine, a plane's turbine. A supersonic silence! On top of the highest skyscrapers, at the air defense installations with their radar systems, the normally strident sirens are silent. Is it because there's no power to make them work? Well in that case… No one knows the reason. Is all this due to lack of foresight?

Groups of anxious onlookers gather at street corners, and especially at the entrances to subway stations, dark caverns emitting stale air where, it is said, more than a million passengers are stuck in the dark between stations, in danger of being asphyxiated. How is this possible? Hasn't anyone ever thought of this? (Who?) As always, it's a case of after the horse has bolted… There were those who assumed the subway would have its own ventilation, a central generator all of its own!… I sense that we are all growing pale.

Other groups form attentively around the lucky people who have brought with them a transistor radio, to listen to the few stations endowed with their own storage batteries; the voices of the broadcasters are solemn and secretly alarmed, and echo through the deathly hush of the streets, advising the stupefied population to remain calm, and trying to explain the as yet inexplicable. But no one—not even the distant government itself—knows what is happening. We find ourselves all of a sudden completely exposed.

A huge swathe of the nation's territory has been deprived of electricity, a strategically vital element, and a crucial factor (without our hitherto realizing it) in our machine-driven existence. Millions of tons of foodstuffs piled up on quays, in hangars, in refrigerated warehouses (that are no longer refrigerated), in stations and airports, in shops and family homes, run the risk of deterioration; the specter of hunger and disease seems to hang over the night. Fortunately summer is almost here! There's no light, no refrigeration, no heating or movement: motion, commotion, locomotion!

Buildings with tens and even hundreds of floors are afflicted by paralysis; electronic doors aren't operating, one can't go in or come out, the elevators don't go up or down, most of them being stuck between floors, with thousands of passengers waiting for help. Who is going to rescue them? No one dares to use stairs, corridors, halls which are plunged in darkness; there is the danger of assault, robbery, rape, murder! We are living in a jungle… And who, without being a climbing acrobat, soldier, policeman or fireman, is going to start climbing thirty or forty floors? The water tanks that crown the buildings are emptying, because the gravity pumps have stopped. The dangers of electricity… Why? Perhaps they were waiting for the water carriers of olden times…? Taps have run dry, and there isn't even a drop. And who has used it all up? One can no longer have a glass of water, make a cup of tea, have a bath, use the restroom, or even wash one's hands. Mineral water… Lucky are those who remembered to put an extra bottle of water in the icebox, where the ice is now melting, dripping persistently in the silence. What if there's a fire?… And the rubbish?! If this thing lasts, it will pile up, fetid and rotting! And the rats, millions of them on the loose!

It's worse than an earthquake. The population feels vulnerable, impotent, unprotected, as if it were under a siege that it had never seen before or experienced. Perhaps it would learn as a result of this. And then we are afflicted by the following idea: what is happening or being planned in the hidden areas, in the ghettoes inhabited by exotic peoples–blacks, yellows, browns, mixed, refugees, illegals, of all origins and colors? Will they take advantage of the darkness (with this moonlight!) to invade the Center, the business areas, the quiet suburbs, to assault, rob, massacre, violate women and innocent children, set fire and get their fill of things? Lord Jesus, have mercy on us, for we cannot bear the burden of our prosperity!

A strange thing, this silence, isn't it? There's no shouting, no stampeding, no conflict, no punching, no aggression. Such is the advantage of terror, for the moment anyway. Peace spills over the City-Emporium. One must conclude that even the thieves and murderers feel intimidated, coerced, inhibited. Perhaps there is a sudden consciousness of God? Of collective danger? There are about twenty thousand policemen (don't even think about the army); what is that when it comes to containing and controlling millions, if terror takes its hold? (But it hasn't happened yet.) Everything moves–whatever or whoever it is that is moving–with a respectfully feudal slowness. Only the buses are working, and the cars of course. As long as there is fuel. As there aren't enough traffic policemen for such an emergency, at the intersections, where vehicles nose in from all sides with timid surprise, volunteers in shirt sleeves, moved by a civic spirit as spontaneous as it is unexpected, but in any case worthy of the greatest praise, equipped with huge flash lights, take on the important role of regulating the flow of traffic. And in the midst of this unprecedented chaos, pedestrians and motorists, usually averse to discipline, passively and almost humbly obey them. How touching this is!

But it is a serious problem: apart from the many millions of cars in the City, almost as many converge on it every day, coming from other cities, neighboring districts and boroughs, and even distant ones, to choke the streets. At this hour, some two million people or more, who have come in for their day's work, for entertainment or to enjoy themselves, are trying to get back home, and the traffic jams are spectacular, truly astronomical. They'll get home, if indeed they get there today, many hours late for their frugal dinner. What will their alarmed families think and say? *Have the Martians landed?* Is it another of Orson Welles's programs? (So far, the only creature remotely resembling a Martian who came, saw and conquered, was Rocky Marciano! The former heavyweight champion.) That was so many years ago. In the City itself, people are going to take hours to cover distances normally covered in minutes. People feel their way along like spiders, colliding gently, without talking. There isn't so much as the sound of a horn! Many cars, on finding the way ahead blocked, turn down streets closed to traffic, or go the wrong way up one-way streets, which makes the confusion and the jam even worse; those who were heading north, turn south, and vice-versa, the same happening to those traveling between east and west. It's no use their studying a compass.

People fear robberies. Shops have closed. Only by candlelight are some counter cafés still open, or counters in cafés. And then everything stops suddenly, as if waiting for goodness knows what.

Night has long since fallen and the Moon shines, like a lookout in the sky. People say the light will return gradually, but only towards the early hours. Apparently some unexpected surge of energy, the equivalent of some sort of waterspout or deep wave originating who knows where or how, suddenly crashed, burning or destroying, or at least temporarily disabling electrical resistance, cables, isolation units, equipment, transformers, and putting power stations out of action. How is such a thing possible? No one has the answers. The crowd passively glides along and slips away. Hours! People climb stairs under the protection of guards who are well armed and equipped with two-way radios. Thank God, at last! *Home sweet home.* One rushes to the kitchen for a drop of coffee or cold tea, maybe a *whiskey-sour*? There's no gas for the stove. A piece of bread and cheese... Standing. Who knows what time we'll have dinner tonight (it's already past eleven) or tomorrow morning? And here we are without any candles in the house! There's depression in the air. We sadly watch the dark, silent City (from the window).

At about three in the morning, the light begins to blink again hesitantly. May the day come soon.

Well, now, when people expected, and I feared that the hysterical crowds would turn the City into an inferno while waiting for something even worse, there wasn't a single fire, accident, robbery or attack, nor even a murder during the entire blackout, and this in a city where there are hundreds of crimes and serious offences reported every day! Only the window of a pawnshop was broken in a poor, crowded area, where this sort of business flourishes along with drug dealing, gambling and prostitution. But nothing was taken. Isn't it strange? Can it be that when men are left to their own devices and fears, like animals obeying ancestral instincts for self-preservation, they display an ability for wisdom and even goodness?... What mysteries the human species feeds upon!

It was later established statistically that the number of children born nine months after that night of terror and solitude, without any other distraction than bed—only the phones were working, but the lines were all congested because of excess calls—was 27.3 percent higher than the usual average. Blessed darkness, holy simplicity! And the lack of water...

Since then too, the number of litigious divorces has inexplicably risen. Could this possibly be because of mistaken identity, people going to the wrong floor, the wrong room, or even the wrong bed?

As you can see, we are prepared for all eventualities.

Retrospection

The City can be summed up in our experience of it. On a number of occasions, hurrying at night along deserted streets,
wrapped in my thoughts, my path has been blocked by a mean-looking
fellow, his arms held wide. I thought my end had come... But no, all my
'assailant' wanted was a nickel or a dime for coffee, and I, heaving a sigh
of relief and with the greatest goodwill, gave him the first coin my fingers touched. We ended up chatting like the best of friends...

From the dentist's waiting room, where I have been waiting for
hours (or years?) for him to attend and torture me, I glimpse the new
two-storey building, a bank, that was put up to replace the old and pomp-
ously named City Opera House, that then became the RKO cinema, on
23rd Street. On the corner, there is a luminous sign that tells me the exact
time and temperature every few minutes, perhaps in order to make me
even more irritable: how much time have I wasted! The area–Chelsea–
was originally a suburb where one went for Sunday lunch, and sixty
years ago was smart and prosperous. Nowadays, it is full of temporary
lodging houses, largely inhabited by noisy Puerto Rican newcomers.
Although I lived virtually round the corner, I didn't go there often. To
the cinema, I mean. One evening, in 36 or 37, I went there with my
wife, as always somewhat against my will, to see Louisa Reiner in an
abominable blockbusting and, worse still, eardrum-piercing film, the

Ziegfeld Follies. The cinema could accommodate twelve to thirteen hundred souls. The cinemas here don't have numbered or reserved seats; films are shown in permanent session, as in the times of our now much-missed Chantecler. First come, first served. There's no tipping either. The *usherette* (a figure that is now tending to disappear as the large cinemas, like the Roxy, Loeb, Paramount and others, close down to give way to smaller cinemas or television "theaters") accompanied us with her *flash-light* to the wide central aisle, and abandoned us there. The stalls were an ocean of ghostly faces, all turned attentively to the tabernacle of seductive images. We walked up and down the interminable rows of comfortable seats set out in an arc like an amphitheater, in search of a place; everywhere was full, like the garage in the Terreiro do Paço at three in the afternoon. We were about to give up, thinking of going up to the huge circles, which were also packed full, or leaving altogether (my preferred solution), when we caught sight of a tiny empty gap in the third row from the back of the stalls; it was as if there were two teeth missing out of a thousand in the gaping chasm of a dragon's mouth. It required courage to undertake such an operation. Before the mirage disappeared, we began to work our way along the row–"Excuse me… Pardon me…"–inconveniencing the cinemagoers, who didn't want to lose a single second of the frenetically dancing legs on the screen. Eventually we were lucky enough to get to the two empty seats, and sat down, both sighing with relief. I folded my old Anglo-Belgian raincoat over my left arm, and was settling down to suffer the musical racket, when I noticed someone on my left vigorously trying to prod me. Surprised, I turned and whispered "did I hurt you?" or some similar apology. My neighbor answered by redoubling his prodding and his threatening growls. He was almost prostrate in his seat, with his thin, pale face propped on his left fist, looking at me with his mouth twisted in a hatred worthy of a gangster film. And then he said in a voice loud enough for those round about to hear: *"Get out of here!"* with a pronunciation typical of his class of person, and which I shall transcribe here: "Guerarahia!" No one gave any sign that they had heard him. The blood rushed through my heart at a hundred and thirty beats, and my instinctive reaction was to get up, fall on him and shower him with punches; nothing would have been easier (relatively speaking!) given his position, and thin as he was, even bearing in mind my lack of weight and boxing ability, and my *fear*. (My wife still wasn't aware of what was going on.) Yes, it was fear that held me back. My situation as an unwelcome foreign visitor was still precarious and didn't allow me the luxury of a fight. What was worse, I had heard of crimes–stabbings and even shootings–in darkened cinemas, which went unpunished, either because no one had heard or seen anything, or (and this was more likely) because no one dared to intervene or get caught up in police business. By this time the Ziegfeld Follies were making a deafening row, and the look on my assailant's face frankly worrying. Was I going to end my days prematurely and ingloriously in the half-light of a cinema? I who aspired to other, more useful feats of prowess? I sweated hot and cold. Deep within me, I was a seething bundle of punches, knife thrusts, screams, stamping feet, spilt blood…

I managed to control myself. I rearranged my raincoat, which deadened the effect of the kicks, and hunched my legs over to the right, saving them from the ruffian's growing fury. I noted some nervousness among the nearest spectators, but none of them complained or even turned to look. There are occasions like this when one is alone in the crowd. When I whispered a couple of words in my wife's ear to tell her what was happening, she was frightened and tried to persuade me to leave. But this was against my principles, quite simply an indignity! If I had to die, better for me to die there alone, at my post! Now it was I who didn't want to leave. And I stayed. And the thing I cannot explain is why it never crossed my mind to ask for help, call an attendant, the police, anyone, so as to have the wrongdoer thrown out. How our timidity, pride, fear of uproar and its consequences makes us put up with so much! I now realized why those two seats had been left free: as insignificant as he was, this *hooligan* had managed to scare off the customers, silencing them and blackmailing them with the terrifying threat of violence! I don't know what political and social conclusions I drew from the incident, but they were certainly abundant, as historical developments were already demonstrating and later confirmed, and it is not difficult to guess what these were.

In the middle of an unfamiliar and indifferent environment, hounded in addition by all manner of personal and impersonal problems and difficulties, I was at the time beginning to be continually on my guard; to feel if not exactly persecuted, at least the object of hostility, to exaggerate a reality that was already painful enough, making me react with irrepressible vehemence at the slightest sign of provocation, antagonism or adversity. I was on the verge of a breakdown and couldn't even imagine what lay in wait. This particular incident, added to so many others, was of the type to produce in me an outburst of defensiveness and the wildest homicidal fantasies. I clenched my fists, and plunged my nails into the palms of my sweating hands.

This wasn't the first, nor would it be last time I wanted to kill or fantasized about doing it. But then I was able to take stock of myself, and realized that, apart from ethical and humanitarian principles, man contains within him negative forces that to some extent inhibit him from indulging in violence: call it prudence, repression, education, or whatever you will. But what use are principles to those who don't suffer from this inhibition, in the blinding impulse of the moment?

Luckily, it wasn't long before a large family to our right got up and left, leaving some seats free. We were therefore able, without loss of face, to move almost to the end of the row. From afar, the hoodlum, now more relaxed, continued to watch me out of the corner of his eye and to mumble insults. He was no doubt one of the many dangerous madmen who are on the loose in this city.

I can't remember whether we saw all the film. I only have the vague memory of one or two close-ups of the whimpering female lead. (What has become of her?) I think we left before the end, stunned by the noise and the upsetting experience. Nor did we ever go back to the RKO on 23rd Street. All because of that memory.

However, you may not believe this, but it pains me not to be able to see it there in front of my eyes, now that the receptionist summons me, as always slightly distorting my name: "Mister Margulies? Surgery C!"

His Majesty the Automobile

That deadly wonder of our age, the Automobile, carrying us further more quickly, has broadened our horizons; but, at the same time, it has increased distances and problems associated with this in respect of transport facilities, enslaving us all the more, and even sometimes destroying the pleasures it promised through the accumulation of traffic, of people, and of the causes of pollution. Thirty or forty years ago, we were just a dozen or so pioneers visiting an isolated beach; nowadays, there are a hundred thousand of us, packed together like grasshoppers or sand flies. And what an effort we had to make to get here! How many hours does the common man have to spend clutching the steering wheel, not to mention the professional? How many people die of heart failure as a result? Our anxiety to arrive, sometimes nowhere in particular, delays our life and hastens our death.

Streets and highways have been turned into race tracks (where this is still possible) and into death ramps; more than five million killed since the beginning of the century, and about ten times more injured or permanently maimed. In the United States, cars cause something in the region of 50,000 deaths every year, the equivalent of 100,000 in France and about the same in Great Britain. The degree of technological know-how doesn't seem to be an attenuating factor: not long ago, West Germany, Yugoslavia and Portugal topped the list for accidents. With some 300,000 motor vehicles for nine million inhabitants over an area of

93,000 square kilometers and the road network that we all know, we killed well over 1,000 people in 1967, which is proportionately many more than in the U.S., with more than 90 million cars for 203 million inhabitants spread over its enormous territorial area, and a road surface equivalent to nearly the whole of Western Europe. If all these cars were on the streets and roads at the same time, they couldn't move–they'd be bumper to bumper.

In the city of New York alone (with its population of seven million) there is one car per one and a half inhabitants; more than 70,000 cars are abandoned every year throughout the country. The great cities, which were made for people to live, work and circulate in, have become monsters of disequilibrium in the way they function, due to the dispersal and concentration of activities that the car has made possible. They are huge garages: cars parked, useless, gathering dust, are lined up in their thousands and millions along the sidewalks, some of them double parked, accumulating rubbish, and making it all the harder to clean, carry out repairs, move goods and effects, for pedestrians to circulate, and for that matter the traffic itself, which is fast by nature. The motorist thinks he has the right to occupy a territory that belongs to everybody, without paying any rent. But there aren't enough garages or parking lots for this hypertrophied mass of immobile transport. A New York surgeon received an emergency call from his hospital, and drove around the neighborhood for three quarters of an hour looking for somewhere to park; by the time he got there, the patient had died.

In the central boulevard of Los Angeles, capital of smog, there was a snarl-up some time ago that left the traffic paralyzed for seven hours. It was noted that of every seven vehicles, only one was carrying a single passenger; that means that if every car carried its full compliment of seven, the jam would only have lasted for one hour. About 75 percent of those using a car don't need it; they would move along more quickly and smoothly on foot, by streetcar, bus or subway, leaving the roads free for those who really need them: doctors, ambulances, firemen, and engineers and workers on urgent business. We save a lot of time, or at least we think we do, only to fritter it away on trivialities. It looks bad to walk! Or it arouses suspicion. You use the car to go to the end of the block to buy a paper or a packet of cigarettes, to have a coffee or a Toxicola. Nothing worth watching on the telly tonight? The indulgent husband says to his yawning wife: "Do you want to go for a drive?" Deserted streets, drizzle, the solitude of the Peugeot... *L'ennui, la noia*, the boredom of this world! And they go home early to bed, disappointed.

The automobile is a toy for adults who maybe haven't had enough childhood. But it provokes neuroses, stress, stomach complaints, gastric ulcers, and heart disease; its emissions aggravate smog, and along with this respiratory illnesses. Certain types of cancer were unknown in parts of Russia before 1920, where the car and its accompanying tarmacked roads were as yet unknown. (Tar is carcinogenic). The incidence of lung cancer has been on the increase for a long time now, with the consumption of fuel oils (and not just cigarettes), and dips when there are restrictions on its consumption, such as occurred during the two world wars. The rate of lung cancer is higher, additionally, among motorists who smoke, and driving merely aggravates the habit. Forty years ago, a professor of social hygiene told us that a traffic policeman in one of America's major cities, after six or seven hours on duty at certain intersections, would faint as a result of intoxication.

Landscapes have been murdered–and who looks at them anyway while traveling at a hundred miles per hour in an ocean of traffic? Apart from the jammed highways and the far greater distances between sources and markets, the cancerous City has swept back vegetable gardens and orchards. Agricultural productivity has been affected, when not destroyed completely, because the devastated soil, covered with rubble and trash, has become as sterile as the plains on the Moon, due to the constant proliferation and widening of roads, many of them unnecessary, except for the bottomless coffers of the oil companies and car manufacturers, two of the largest and most irresistible empires in world business. Oil and gasoline spilled into the oceans constitute a serious threat to marine life, to the fishing industry, and to those who live or spend their holidays by the beach. And the Russians and others even complain about the lack of motor vehicles.

We rush around like demented ants, in opposite directions, and with no destination, along these wonders of modern engineering and enemies of mankind, the freeways. It's enough to see them from the air! Governments, states, municipalities, pressured by powerful interests, devote vast budgets to roads and bridges, extorted from taxpayers, some of whom don't even own an automobile or are their victims–all of us are!–but who are powerless to prevent this massacre or to put its culprits, true "steering wheel murderers" out of circulation. To be truthful, it must be said that the responsibilities of the motorist in the United States are huge: the pedestrian is, in principle, always right.

But the motor car isn't just an occasionally lethal weapon on the road; it has become an escape and a gratification, the catharsis or sublimation, at a basic level, for repressed aggressiveness, stifled rebellion, underlying sadism, not to mention suicidal tendencies, more conspicuous among the young who are by nature more indifferent to life, or more blind to its value, if they value it at all: which is why, from the era of the Greek phalanges up until the "arditti" and other warlike organizations of our modern demagogies, the young have always fallen voluntary victims of this "disregard for life". This is why the cost of motor insurance in the United States is prohibitive for those between the ages of 17 and 22, the age group that has the highest rate of serious motoring accidents.

The Automobile is also a morbid extension of personality and sensitivity; the slightest contact, scratch or dent in the paint of its bodywork or chrome fittings, induces reactions that make insults or knife thrusts pale into insignificance; if someone crosses the road in front of me and forces me to slow down, overtakes me or "steals" my precious parking space–I leap out of my car, fuming and with fists clenched, ready to insult, assault, even kill, as is often the case, the transgressor of my most sacred "rights". The car has turned men into truly mechanized, metallic insects, brainless spider crabs, heartless, isolated from each other by the carapace of two tons of steel-plate with an engine and four wheels, capable of crushing bones, flesh and nerves, which they climb into and drive (or are driven) without seeing their fellow men: with the same absence of feelings, the same fury, indifference or hostility with which they would move among their enemies or through conquered territory. Could this perhaps be because driving is one of the few freedoms left to the species, caught in the trap of its own technology that reduces man to the level of a glorified robot?

To crush or be crushed, that is the question; there is a constant duel between motorists or between them and the pedestrian, who views them with a hatred that would only be satisfied, as it would among dogs, with the hair of the same animal.

The Black Man and Mr. Harding

Warren Gamaliel Harding was President (but strictly speaking didn't govern) from 1920 to 1923. Debonair and well-spoken, God-fearing, conservative, uncultured, isolationist as the spirit of the age demanded, he climbed every rung on the political career ladder, from a small provincial newspaper in Marion (Ohio) to the White House. Freed from European capital, America was determinedly entering on the path of expansion and endless prosperity, to the sound of the clarion call of John Felipe de Souza (with a z), in opposition to the pessimistic, expatriate literature of Dos Passos, Hemingway and Scott Fitzgerald. *America beautiful, America forever!* Until when? 1921 was a year of severe crisis. There had been others. The impotent Mister Harding saw the coterie that had enabled him to be elected for Lincoln's *Grand Old* Republican Party drown in scandals. Bribery, embezzlement, the sale of jobs and contracts… Some of his closest collaborators ended up behind bars. Justice was done!–it was important for people to be aware of this.

The President was alarmed, and rushed off on a tour of the country, accompanied by his wife and a large retinue. In Alaska, a mysterious coded telegram, the content of which was never revealed, caused him sudden embarrassment. Exhausted and sick, he went and died in San Francisco on August 2, 1923. There was talk of a conspiracy and poisoning; he was found to have committed adultery and to have an illegitimate daughter, just imagine the horror! Something seems to have grown rotten in the kingdom of Puritanism. Men preferred to keep quiet. His biography would only come to light some forty years later.

And those poor forgotten folk the Blacks: what were they asking, begging for, expecting? In the name of the Constitution: "All men are born free and equal." Some more, others less… There's no evidence that Mr. Harding did anything. What could he do? The South (democratic) threatened on the sidelines. And then the Blacks, if we give them a hand… In order to emancipate them, the free and generous America had embarked on the Civil War: five years of fighting (1860-65), 250,000 dead, incalculable destruction, the South burned to cinders and reduced to a colony of the North. After "King Cotton" came the reign of the carpet-baggers, agents of the banking and industrial capitalism of the North. (They were called this because of the bags made out of carpet material they carried with them). A group of eminent Blacks met with President Lincoln in the White House: "What was their future going to be?" The Emancipator was exemplary in his honesty: "This is a nation of white men. You will never know equality here. Go back to Africa, or look for a country where you may settle in Latin America." Where were they to go? This was their land. They had been born here, the children of slaves brought here by force, and at the will of their masters. They stayed. The *"Back to Africa"* movement, that had had some popularity, was to gradually die down. Liberia, which had been created out of a purchase, had led to the conquest of Africans by black Americans: for the benefit of the Firestone Rubber Company above all. (Paul Robeson would make a mediocre film in the 1930s, condemning the Return to Africa.)

After the Civil War, during Reconstruction (1866-77), many Southern Blacks were elected to Congress. But between 1901 and 1928, there was only one Black congressman: a silent minority of one. The Ku Klux Klan (1866), backed by harsh laws and customs, had turned "Lynch" into a weapon of intimidation. Keeping Blacks in their place became the order of the day. In whatever way possible. The right to vote and to citizenship, guaranteed by the constitutional amendments of 1865 and 1868, became a dead letter. The courts, including the Supreme Court, washed their hands of the matter. The Harding era was therefore a bleak one for Afro-Americans.

It is estimated that in the first decade of this century, there were some 900 lynchings, almost all of them in the South. Even in 1935-36, I heard of half a dozen; and I witnessed the noisy demonstrations in favor of the "Scottsboro Boys", Angelo Herndon, and other martyrs and victims of persecution. Blacks commanded a higher level of awareness throughout the country. It was round about then that I published (in *O Diabo*) the following verses: *"A Negro dances in the cabaret/ with an all white smile/stuck between his teeth like an imaginary fruit..."*

Although they never stopped showing their discontent and resisting–apart from one or two limited but famous rebellions: G. Prosser, Nat Turner, Douglass and others (John Brown was white and came later)– the slaves were surprisingly cautious: there was nothing like the slave maroons, such as Palmares in Brazil! They sought refuge in nostalgia, spirituals, Christianity, an impenetrable reserve and dignity (the fewer disputes with Whites the better!), and caricature that they then gave to vaudeville and the cinema: superstition, fear, childishness, clumsiness... indolence! Their preachers, singers and athletes were, however, always extraordinary. (How I would like to tell you here about Mathilda, Tom, Mr. James and other black people I knew!)

Even before Abolition, Blacks, whether slave or free, fled north; there was the famous underground railway. From a black population of 800,000 in 1790–one fifth of the total population, 90% of them in the South, where cotton was the main cash crop–they had increased to 10 million in 1920, 85% of them still in the South, and still tied to the land. Nowadays, there are 21 million, 11% of the population, less than 60% of them in the South. Masters favored slave breeding because it was profitable. First, cotton and misery, then freedom, caused them to multiply, always with the collaboration of Whites between the sheets. More than 70% of North American Blacks are in fact mixed. Many also have Indian blood.

With the First World War, religion and industry encouraged the migration of some two million Blacks to the North. The competition that this limitless workforce represented–Blacks were used above all as "scabs" or strike-breakers on lower wages–provoked hostility from industrial workers, who were mainly European in origin. On the other hand, these were "foreigners" as far as Blacks were concerned... Some of the big employers and the Labor Unions preferred the immigrant–sober, hard-working, ambitious and obedient or conformist–to the Black, handicapped by historical conditioning, ignorance and latent rebelliousness. Restrictions on immigration, with the inevitable unemployment caused by the crisis, and lack of housing, aggravated hostility. Meanwhile, the black ghetto, the scourge of the great urban centers, spread, bringing with it its accompanying misery: crime, drugs, gambling, vagrancy, prostitution, venereal diseases, illegitimate children, high mortality... Just as it still does today! The specter grew, and with it the problem of conscience. According to the black novelist James Baldwin, the American nation suffers from a feeling of guilt that gnaws away inside it, as a caterpillar might inside a shining fruit. Parallel to this, Blacks suffer from a tragic complex of inferiority (and ugliness), which is reflected in the vast majority of crimes committed by Blacks, which are against Blacks themselves. And the black woman, a victim of the sexual domination of the white man, becomes in turn a double victim of the black man, a target for his exploitation, jealousy and scorn...

With the Second World War, all this got worse, and then came the street battles. Dozens of Blacks were massacred in the pogrom at Detroit, the capital of the automobile. Blacks threatened to march on Washington, like the unemployed in the time of Hoover, to demand compensation. Roosevelt launched his Executive Order against discrimination in the industries of war; it was no more than a gesture, but it marked the beginning of a new era. The Central Committee of the Industrial Organization (CIO), more progressive than the A.F. of L. (American Federation of Labor), opened its doors to them. At the time, the Communist Party advocated a separate State for Blacks in the Union, an idea that didn't command much support, but that has recently been revived by some organizations. The (black) snowball got bigger, and rolled. Blacks no longer asked, as they had in Harding's time; they demonstrated, protested, fought. Eisenhower in 1955, and John F. Kennedy in 1961, strengthened the equality of Blacks in industry. The Supreme Court eventually decreed educational integration. Colleges, such as the City University of New York, allow them free enrolment. (Nowadays, it has about 200,000 students.) There is equality of pay in the established professions. The ghetto has overflowed, and is invading the suburbs, previously the refuge of the moneyed classes. There is still resistance, evasiveness, even violence in some sectors, but nothing can hold back the flood. Even in the South, the bulwark of *Apartheid*, school integration is becoming the norm, and Blacks are standing for election. The Puerto Ricans in the cities, hitherto a rival group, are joining them in their revindications. (These new arrivals, in some areas of work, are better paid than native Blacks.) The police, proverbially harsh in their repression of white students, are becoming more moderate, and avoid violent confrontation. There are a number of forces working for a peaceful and progressive solution to the problem. Blacks are casting off their inferiority complex. Nowadays, we see Nordic blondes in our streets flaunting the fruits of their unions with black men... In effect, the solution seems to lie in conviviality, love, intimacy—just as the sociologist, Professor Wagley, thought he saw in Brazil. The black vote is now influential in both large and even small cities. The proponents of violence are losing ground... although there are those who have placed their hopes for the Revolution in the prison population.

The road still to be traveled is certainly a long one; unemployment among Blacks continues to be twice the level of that among Whites; their infant mortality is far higher, and far lower their individual life expectancy. Lack of training and of a culture of work still limits them to more menial jobs. But is there a sudden and total solution to any problem? Progress has been such over the last fifty years that one is justified in talking of a "revolution". And what nation, conscious of its own ethnic individuality, would accept without fear such a worrying presence? For it is not just a social and economic, or even racial question, but also a clash of identities, of cultures, of *ways of life*, that places the moral equilibrium of the nation at risk. Only those who don't have the problem in their own home can talk of easy solutions. The homogeneity of a multiracial nation of continental proportions has never been achieved overnight. When will we stop thinking in *slogans*, abstractions, fixed but wooly ideas, and face up to reality and think objectively, using our own head?

Poor, forgotten Mr. Harding! And how old were we, what dreams, what illusions did we have fifty years ago? How many disappointments have we suffered since then?

(Written at the invitation of the *Diário de Lisboa* to commemorate its 50ᵗʰ anniversary. This newspaper, in its first issue in 1921, had published a telegram from Washington, giving the news of the meeting between black leaders and President Harding. This was my comment.)

Books Published by Gávea-Brown

Portuguese Studies

1. Onésimo T. Almeida, ed., *José Rodrigues Miguéis – Lisbon in Manhattan*
2. Francisco C. Fagundes, *A Poet's Way With Music: Humanism in Jorge de Sena's Poetry*
3. Eduardo Lourenço, *This Little Lusitanian House: Essays on Portuguese Culture.* Trans. by Ronald W. Sousa
4. George Monteiro, ed., *The Man Who Never Was: Essays on Fernando Pessoa*
5. Nelson H.Vieira, ed., *Roads to Today's Portugal*

Portuguese American Series

6. Sam Beck, *Manny Almeida's Ringside Lounge*
7. Richard Beale Davis, *The Abbé Corrêa In America, 1812-1820.* Pref. by Gordon S.Wood. Afterword by Léon Boudon
8. Maria A. Duarte and Ronald W. Sousa, *Reading the Harper: On a Portuguese Immigrant Poem from California, 1901*
9. Francisco C. Fagundes, ed., *Ecos de Uma Viagem: Em honra de Eduardo Mayone Dias*
10. Onésimo T. Almeida and Alice R. Clemente, eds., *George Monteiro: The Discreet Charm of a Portuguese-American Scholar*
11. José Rodrigues Miguéis, *The Polyhedric Mirror – Tales of American Life.* Trans. by David Brookshaw

Poetry

12. Onésimo T. Almeida, ed., *The Sea Within – A Selection of Azorean Poetry.* Trans. by George Monteiro
13. Eugénio de Andrade, *The Shadow's Weight.* Trans. by Alexis Levitin
14. Thomas J. Braga, *Portingales*
15. Emanuel Félix, *The Possible Journey, Poetry (1965-1992).* Trans. by John M. Kinsella
16. José Martins Garcia, *Temporal*
17. João Teixeira de Medeiros, *Do Tempo e de Mim.* Ed. by Onésimo T. Almeida
18. George Monteiro, *The Coffee Exchange*
19. Fernando Pessoa, *Self–Analysis and Thirty Other Poem.* Trans. by George Monteiro
20. Jorge de Sena, *In Crete with the Minotaur and Other Poems.* Trans. by George Monteiro
21. Miguel Torga, *Iberian Poem.* Trans. by George Monteiro

Fiction

22. Camilo Castelo Branco, *Doomed Love (a family memoir)*. Trans. by Alice R. Clemente
23. *Visions of China: Stories from Macau*. Various authors. Trans. by David Brookshaw
24. Alice R. Clemente, ed., *Sweet Marmalade, Sour Oranges: Contemporary Portuguese Women's Fiction*. Various translators
25. Vitorino Nemésio, *Stormy Isles: An Azorean Tale*. Trans. by Francisco C. Fagundes
26. Dias de Melo, *Dark Stones*. Trans. by Gregory McNab
27. José Rodrigues Miguéis, *Steerage and Ten Other Stories*. Ed. by George Monteiro. Various translators

Theater

28. Bernardo Santareno, *The Judgment of Father Martinho – A Dramatic Narrative in Two Acts*. Trans. by Celso de Oliveira
29. Bernardo Santareno, *The Promise*. Trans. by Nelson H. Vieira

Autobiography

30. Francisco C. Fagundes, *Hard Knocks: An Azorean-American Odyssey*